Latinas in
ARCHITECTURE
and Allies
VOL. II

Stories of raising the 1% one Latina at a time

ALICIA PONCE, AIA, NCARB, LEED AP BD+C

LATINAS IN ARCHITECTURE AND ALLIES VOL. 2

This book is a compilation of stories from numerous people who have each contributed a chapter and is designed to provide inspiration to our readers.

It is sold with the understanding that the publisher and the individual authors are not engaged in the rendering of psychological, legal, accounting or other professional advice. The content and views in each chapter are the sole expression and opinion of its author and not necessarily the views of Fig Factor Media, LLC.

For more information visit:
APMonarch | www.apmonarch.com
Arquitina |www.arquitina.org
Fig Factor Media | www.figfactormedia.com

Cover Design by DG Marco Álvarez
Layout by LDG Juan Manuel Serna Rosales

Printed in the United States of America

ISBN: 978-1-957058-90-0

To Mami for giving me your unconditional love every single day. Eres todo.

"It matters not how strait the gate, how charged with punishment the scroll, I am the master of my fate, I am the captain of my soul." – William Ernest Henley

TABLE OF CONTENTS

ACKNOWLEDGMENTS

I come as one, but I stand as ten thousand.

–Maya Angelou

To the Women who are opening doors for others and the Men that hold them open. We see you. To the people that don't. We see you too.

Publishing Latinas in Architecture and Allies Volume II would not have been possible without the success of Volume I. Oftentimes we think no one is watching, but the truth is the co-authors have inspired many readers across the country from all walks of life to be the change they seek. Your personal story is connecting with someone else right now. What may have seemed impossible for others is now possible. Thank you co-authors of Volume I, Claudette Soto, Gabriela Arreola Ceferin, Karina Ruiz, Ingedia K. Sanchez, Lourdes Mesa Gonzalez, Beatriz Eugenia Lopez Alzate, Yiselle Santos Rivera, Michelle Joan Galiano, Frida Araceli Palacios Acevedo, Maria Laguarda-Mallo, Natalie Soledad Ramirez, Rosa Y. Ortiz, Raquel Guzman Geara, Maria A. Pellot Peraza, Patricia Saldaña Natke, Graciela Carrillo, Karen Garcia, and Yanet Garcia.

To the trailblazing Women who have so graciously contributed their thoughts and experiences in the introduction; Carmen Suero, Margaret Young Zirkel, Kavitha Matthew, Tiara Hughes, Evelyn M. Lee and Mani Helene Ardalan Farhadi, thank you. Your work does not go unnoticed. Your voice does not go unheard.

To the powerhouse Arquitina planning committee, Alzira Maldonado Protsishin, Raquel Guzman Geara, Jessica Adetoro, Delly Yaker, Veronica Pochet, Patricia Centeno, Natalie Ramirez and Laura Nuñez, thank you for your countless hours of dedication to meticulously plan the cohorts. You are most definitely lifting as we climb!

Thank you to the organizations and firms who have shown continued support for Arquitina and our mission, Epstein Global Foundation, HMC Designing Futures Foundation, KPF, AIA Chicago, AIA Arizona, AIA National, AIA San Francisco, AIA Long Island. Arquitina welcomes more supporters and speaking opportunities.

Thank you, Fig Factor Media, for your continued support and giving wings to so many of our dreams.

Thank you to my grandparents, (QEPD), Manuel and Felicitas Sanchez who created such a supporting and loving family. Who planted the seeds of determination, joy, and unity. You taught us that even the smallest amount of faith can have the biggest impact.

Thank you to my husband Cesar and our kids Emilio and Paz. I love you.

FOREWORD
By Carol Ross Barney

I didn't always want to be an architect.

I saw myself as a painter or perhaps a sculptor since I loved making and repairing... almost anything. John F. Kennedy was elected the year I started high school and I don't think that any 13-year-old could resist the clarion call to service in his inaugural address: *"My fellow citizens of the world: ask not what America will do for you, but what together we can do for the freedom of man."*

I decided that being a painter was not enough to save the world. I didn't know any architects, but I reasoned that designing great and equitable spaces was something an architect would do. I have never looked back. I am as challenged and as heartened by the power of design to improve the quality of human life as I was sixty years ago. I love being an architect.

I have been fortunate to always have great mentorship and support. My mother, who confessed to dreaming of being the first woman president of the United States, was delightfully blind to gender roles as were the Sisters who taught at my all girls Catholic High School. So, as I entered the School of Architecture at the University of Illinois at Urbana Champaign, I was blissfully unaware that I was one of only five women in my school. At the time there were only 400 registered women architects in the United States an infinitesimally small number representing less than 1% of the profession.

My first design teacher told me that women shouldn't be architects and gave me a failing grade. An appeal to the Dean turned it into a "D," but I still ended up on academic probation. If they were hoping to dissuade me, it made me more determined. Five years later, I was one of three women graduating in my class of 100.

I found my first job in Chicago by searching the want ads under "Help wanted—Men." When I landed an interview at a major firm, the interviewer gave me a typing test to make sure I could fill in as a receptionist or secretary if needed. I didn't get the job because I was, and still am, a dismal typist.

I started one position on my 23rd birthday and had to endure the managing partner demanding a "birthday kiss" as part of my orientation.

So, that was the beginning and, if I am being completely honest, Architecture has never loved me as much I love Architecture. What doesn't kill you makes you stronger and the joy and fulfillment of making space has wiped out any disappointment or regret. Every day, every drawing, every project is a new challenge.

My personal story is not special or unique. Strong, brave, and persistent women doing important things have progressively been changing the face of the profession. According to the American Institute of Architects, currently 17% of registered architects are women. Progress has been constant and excruciatingly slow, but I believe it would be even slower without the collaborative and supportive sisterhood of women architects I have come to rely on.

In 1921, Elizabeth Martini ran an announcement in a local newspaper stating, *"Only Girl Architect Lonely: Wanted—to meet all of the women architects in Chicago to form a club."* Although Martini was still the only licensed female architect in the city, draftswomen responded and they formed the Chicago Women's Drafting Club, supporting and advocating for each other.

While I was working at my first job, I received a postcard from Gertrude Lempp Kerbis. It was an invitation, *"Come and meet other female architects about coalition [...] all invited."* On January 12, 1974, at that meeting in Gertrude's office, Chicago Women in Architecture was formed to combat the isolation felt by women architects at the time. Over the years, CWA has successfully worked on the issues of lack of recognition for contributions, lack of access to public projects, lack of professional support for the challenges of raising children or caring for aging parents, lack of pay equity, and lack of sensitivity to gender differences while providing a supportive coalition for women architects.

Which brings me to the wonderful book you now hold in your hands. *Latinas in Architecture Volume 2* is the work of my good friend and frequent collaborator, Alicia Ponce. In addition to leading a growing and innovative architectural practice, Alicia is the founder of Arquitina, a professional leadership and licensure initiative for Latinas in the field of Architecture.

In 1988, I was appointed to an AIA Committee to study the status of women in the profession. We decided to organize an exhibit celebrating the 100th anniversary of the election of the first woman AIA member, Louise Blanchard Bethune of Buffalo, New York. The exhibit was titled "That Exceptional One."

In the 1950's, New York Life Insurance Company published a series of public service pamphlets to help young people make career choices. For "Should you be an Architect," Pietro Belluschi, Dean of Architecture at MIT and AIA Gold Medalist was interviewed. When asked about women being architects, Belluschi said, *"I cannot, in whole conscience, recommend architecture as a profession for girls. I know some women who have done well at it, but the obstacles are so great that it takes an exceptional girl to make a go of it. If she insisted on becoming an architect, I would try to dissuade her. If then, she was still determined, I would give her my blessing—she could be that exceptional one."*

Alicia and her Aquitina cohorts are the VERY exceptional ones, just by numbers alone. Latina architects represent less than 1% of registered architects in the United States. Since its inception in 2020, Arquitina has initiated an ambitious mentorship program to support Latina licensure candidates. The publication of Latinas in Architecture was a watershed moment when the stories of individual women were introduced to the world. It is a very intimate and personal view of the challenges that women architects, especially Latinas face today. It is recognition of their passion and accomplishment. I am very honored and proud to be writing to you about *Volume 2*.

When Louise Bethune was admitted as AIA's first female member, her colleagues toasted her saying "Here's to the Lady from New York. May there be many more!" *Latinas in Architecture*

Volume 1 is subtitled "Stories of raising the 1% one Latina at a time." I know that this is the start of many, many more.

In sisterhood,

Carol Ross Barney | FAIA, Hon. ASLA

Design Principal and Founder

Photo Credits:
Boehm Photography
by John Boehm

BIOGRAPHY

Carol Ross Barney, FAIA, HASLA has been in the vanguard of civic space design since founding Ross Barney Architects in 1981. With a career that spans nearly 50 years, Carol has made significant contributions to the built environment, the profession, and architectural education. From the early days in the United States Peace Corps planning National Parks in Costa Rica to recent collaborations with City Governments, Carol has relentlessly advocated that excellent design is a right, not a privilege.

Her body of work, being almost exclusively in the public realm, represents this ethos and occupies a unique place within the panorama of contemporary architecture.

Carol's projects vary in type and scale, but always uphold a deep commitment to the quality of life. This commitment manifests into spaces that enrich the metropolitan experience; buildings that are environmental stewards, embodying and showcasing sustainability; and spaces that inspire young, curious minds to learn, invent, and break boundaries.

At the forefront for equity in the architectural profession, Carol has long sought to move beyond her gender as a contributing factor or hindrance to success. But it's not enough just to blaze the trail, Carol continually teaches, mentors, and empowers young architects to contribute their ideas and designs to progress the profession.

A native Chicagoan, Carol is the mother of three sons and grandmother of Kai and Han.

INTRODUCTION
by Alicia Ponce

It's been two years since Latinas in Architecture Volume I was published. The book has been embraced by architecture firms, Universities, and bookstores across the country. I admit I didn't know what to expect but the impact of our stories has caused a rustling of the feathers in a very, very good way. What I mean by this is that Latinas in architecture are holding their heads higher, their eyes spark a bit brighter and the determination to become leaders in the field of architecture is bolder. After Volume I was released, I've been invited to speak about the book both locally and nationally by those that are seeking transformative change in their organizations. More importantly, they are open to learning, listening and growth as well as creating diverse, equitable and inclusive opportunities for Latinas. I had the privilege of meeting many more Latinas across the country on their journey to licensure. Whether they have five years of experience or thirty-five, they have all said, "Thank you for noticing me".

Interesting data points I have personally been following over the last 20 years are the annual reports published by NCARB (National Council of Architectural Registration Boards) and the AIA (American Institute of Architects). Year after year, the reports showed Latinas as less than one percent of licensed architects in the US. As of 2022, the numbers show we are 1.7%. I found this to be quite peculiar yet exciting. Are we moving the needle after 160 years of AIA existence? Are we, Latinas, and Women of Color speaking up more? In short, the answer is YES we are.

Additionally, the AIA has a distinguished designation known as the "AIA College of Fellows" or FAIA. This designation is awarded to less than 3% of AIA members and is the AIA's highest honor, recognizing those who have made notable contributions to the field in one of six areas: Design & Preservation, Practice, Leadership, Service, Education & Research. If Latinas are 1.7% of licensed architects in the US and a lesser percentage are firm owners or principals, how many have been elevated to FAIA by their peers? How many Latinas are on track to FAIA status? I don't know, but I'm on a mission to find out.

Carmen Suero, an Afro-Latina from the Dominican Republic and Principal of Good Project Company in Los Angeles, feels that, "As women of color in a predominantly male profession, we often face a shortage of mentors and role models who understand the complexities of our experiences and can offer guidance and support to propel our careers forward. This lack of guidance hinders our access to crucial resources such as professional development opportunities, funding, and networks and restricts our ability to achieve our full potential."

To share a glimpse of the experience of non-Latinas in architecture, I reached out to extraordinary leading architects lighting the torch for others. I met Mani Helene Ardalan Farhadi in the fall of 2022. She is an Iranian-American architect with 35 years of experience and is a Senior Facilities Planner at Stanford University, School of Medicine. When I spoke with Mani, I wasn't surprised to find that we share the same frustrations when it comes to representation in the profession and what it takes for us to reach a leading role in design, planning or project management. However challenging our experiences may be, we both are passionate about helping others. Mani shared, "In the past decade, these advocacy groups (NOMA, Equity by Design, Arquitina, and others) representing minorities have made enormous strides in raising awareness. I co-founded a newer niche group called BIBI (Banous in Building Industry), with Lili Etessam in 2015, designed for Iranian women in planning, architecture, interiors, landscape, engineering, construction, and academia. Currently we have 150 members across North America, with monthly virtual gatherings, to mentor and support one another as we navigate career decisions. As an Iranian identity group, we face stereotype and prejudice. By coming together, we amplify each other and build self-confidence. These days, we are motivated more than ever by the women-led revolution in Iran, as brave females fight oppression. Here in the US, because of our representation, more Iranian women have joined the AIA, and our hope is to increase those who will become licensed."

My dear friend, Tiara Hughes, member of NOMA (National Organization of Minority Architects) is a black female architect in Chicago who says, "Design firms and the industry at large have discussed 'equality of opportunity' as a remedy to pay gaps, gender inequalities, and systemic racism in America.

Equality is not the solution; many women have experienced decades of economic and emotional trauma stemming from dress code policies, lesser gender-specific roles, pay inequity, and more. These burdens are carried in the workplace, which means 'equality' by providing employees with the same resources for success without acknowledging their gender-specific troubles, fails us all. Acknowledgment has occurred to an extent with the recognition of some of our historic trailblazers, but our country's collective mindset has to shift from equality to equity. Equity means meeting people where they are and addressing their needs accordingly." She adds that her personal experience, such as curriculum and textbooks not including the work of black architects along with her passion for advocacy led her to establish a global platform called FIRST 500 in 2018. Tiara continues to say, "As the founder and executive director of FIRST 500, I travel the country to raise awareness of black women architects throughout history and their contributions to the built environment. These women inspire and motivate black women to get licensed and complete their architecture education today. I'm proud of meeting the milestone of 500 licensed black women architects, but this is only the beginning. We have a lot of work to do to cultivate the next 500 black women architects living in the US and the world." With 10 years of experience, Tiara has quickly become an influential role model for black female architects and one to keep watching.

By far, one of the most heartwarming encounters I've had was at the 2022 AIA Women's Leadership Summit during our lunch break. I was sitting at a table of eight women having a casual conversation. We were just getting to know each other when suddenly a young Asian architect asked if I was the creator of the Latinas in Architecture book to which I replied, "yes". Next, there was an unexpected emotional exchange of "thank you" and "lift as you climb" responses. That moment made the "movement" really sink in for me. I was scheduled to speak on a panel that afternoon in front of 750 people and this encounter flooded me with nerves, because I realized that the stories in the book are truly and authentically connecting with the readers inspiring them on their personal journey in architecture, Latina or not.

During speaking engagements, White males in leadership ask me, "How does someone like me help?" I think it's a great question to ask, especially in a public setting where other leaders in the industry are listening. By leaders, I mean people who are in the position of power to make decisions to hire, to pay equitably, to sponsor Latinas, to advocate for Latinas in design and put Latinas on a track to Director and Principal at their firm. This notion holds true for Women of Color generally.

With 20 years of experience, Kavitha Matthew who is South Asian (Indian) and Global Diversity Director at KPF, shares that "affinity bias is rampant and has led to a historically white male field to remain that way. Women of color who enter the field are often paid less than their white male counterparts and are less likely to be promoted. Exposing these inequities and embracing more transparent processes are ways to begin to dismantle the status quo."

I met Chinese architect and entrepreneur Evelyn M. Lee, FAIA, NOMA, when she invited me to speak on the podcast "Practice Disrupted" with Evelyn Lee and Je'Nen Chastain. With 120 episodes and counting, they "set out to illuminate the future of the profession to help architects remain relevant and valuable in a changing world." When asked about why she thinks it's important to be equitable, inclusive, and diverse in architecture, Evelyn shares, "Inclusive spaces break down barriers and facilitate equal access, empowering people with varying abilities to maneuver through the built environment easily. Ultimately, prioritizing equity and diversity in architecture creates vibrant, inclusive communities that enrich society."

For Latinas, it is more common, than not, to be advised to "put your head down and work hard". "Don't ask too many questions and do your very best." "Si se puede!" It is without a doubt that our supportive families and pride in our heritage are huge motivators to go out there and do well despite being painfully misunderstood because of our background and gender. Being "different" in a White male dominated industry innately confronts Women in deep rooted establishments.

In April of 2023, I had the great pleasure of meeting architect Margaret Young Zirkel as she received the Lifetime Achievement Award, and I received the Breaking Glass Award by the Chicago Women in Architecture. I learned, yet again, there is still a long way to go on this mission to go above and beyond the 1% of licensed Latina architects in the US. Our challenges as Women and Women of Color are similar whether we are in the year 2023 or 1953! Margaret shared, "My family immigrated to Chicago from southern Germany in 1953. Only my father spoke a little English. I was 12 and my sister 9. The local Public School (in a Bohemian & Polish neighborhood) wanted nothing to do with us, because of our lack of English and because of lingering animosity towards anything or anyone German and so soon after WWII. However, with the help of the Catholic Church school across the street, I quickly acquired sufficient command of my new language to be placed into the 6th grade and from then on it was smooth sailing. I fit in but felt it necessary to not speak of my heritage until many years later."

"So, without personally feeling or understanding any other inequities around me, I just plowed ahead with stubbornness and determination. My German heritage and my parents demanded that I work hard, do the very best I could and take my responsibilities seriously, whether in school, at my jobs or in my life, and without regard of established limitations like being a woman in a man's field. The rest is history, and I am closing in on my 82nd birthday."

Margaret's experience is so familiar to the women and our allies in this book. Despite adversity and oftentimes feeling unwelcome, we thrive, and we excel. We keep moving forward even if we are pulled and pushed back.

Once again, my request is that you read with an open heart and open mind. Share our stories and together, let's continue to move that stubborn little needle and lift as we climb!

BIOGRAPHY

A proud daughter of Mexican immigrants, Alicia Ponce is the Founder and Principal of APMonarch, a Chicago based Architecture firm. Under Alicia's direction, the firm provides architectural services, sustainability consulting and community engagement for projects throughout the Midwest and Mexico. Her expertise and passion to design healthy buildings and equitable communities creates architecture that is ambitious, thoughtful, and healthy. APMonarch provides these services to diverse sectors including Commercial, Higher-Education, Civic, Healthcare, and Retail.

Alicia refers to APMonarch as the pollinator of the built environment designing healthy environments that look good, feel good and perform great! The firm's promise is to build zero carbon architecture. A registered architect in Illinois and Wisconsin, Alicia has over 25 years of architecture and sustainability experience and is a graduate from the University of Illinois at Urbana-Champaign.

In 2020, Alicia founded Arquitina, a national 501(c)3 organization with a mission to raise the one percent of licensed Latina architects in the U.S and she is the creator of the award-winning book Latinas in Architecture Vol I. In 2022, she received the Landmarks Illinois Influencer award and the Maestro Leader Award by Latinos Magazine. Alicia is a Board Member for United Way Metro Chicago and is an appointed Commissioner with Chicago Landmarks. She is happily married to Cesar and a very happy Mami to Emilio and Paz.

ALICIA PONCE, AIA, NCARB, LEED AP
aponce@apmonarch.com
LinkedIn: Alicia Ponce Architect

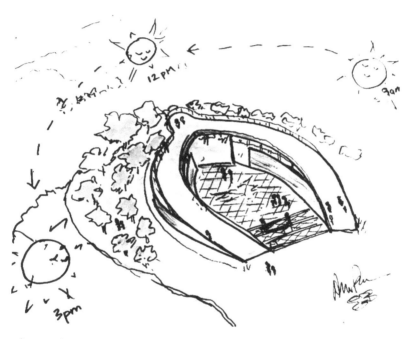

An initial concept sketch of the Instituto Desarrollo Amazing Aguascalientes
(IDAA) — a beautiful center for the youth in Mexico with a structural concept
of coming out of the earth, made from the earth.

Author Stories

MONICA RODRIGUEZ

I am starting my story with the backstory of my mom and dad, Amparo and Armando Rodriguez. Coming from humble lives in the small town of Tepetongo, Zacatecas in the 40s and 50s, going to college or university and having a professional career was never an option for them. My mom got as far as finishing *preparatoria,* and my dad was pulled out of school after the sixth grade since he could read and write, and that was good enough for my grandfather.

My parents married young, my mom was nineteen and my dad was twenty, and lived on a ranch outside of town for about a year and a half. Feeling that they could provide a better life for their growing family in the United States, they made the decision to move.

My parents immigrated to California as permanent residents in 1963 with already one child in tow, my sister, Leticia. Both my parents worked physically demanding jobs all their lives and were able to provide for their five children as best they could. While my parents never specifically told my siblings and me to do good in school, stay out of trouble, be respectful of others and get good jobs, it was ingrained in us. We didn't need to hear it to know that is what they wanted of us.

Looking back at my life from childhood to now and at my journey as an architect, what I see and recognize as the most important thing is all the support and guidance I had throughout my entire life. I have had so many mentors and allies that have helped me along the way. By far my biggest allies have always been my mother and father.

My mom and dad had the joy of their fifth child being the most obnoxiously independent short-tempered daughter they could have ever hoped for, me. The story goes that as soon as I had enough hand-and-eye coordination to feed myself, I would not let anyone feed me and I'd throw a tantrum if anyone tried it. I'd make the biggest mess of course and I'd mark the end of my meal by placing the bowl on the top of my head, like a hat.

Recently my dad reminded me of that story and said, "Mija, tu siempre has sido independiente, desde chiquita cuando te ponías el plato en tu cabeza. No tienes que cambiarte por nadie, eres perfecta, así te queremos." My mom and dad recognizing me, seeing me for who I am since birth, is special to me. It laid the path for life that I've made for myself and I appreciate that support from them every day.

My first memory of wanting to be an architect is unusual I think, and I often joke about it, but it's a true story. I was around six or seven years old. It was summer break, and I was at home with my brothers and sisters. My oldest sister, Leticia put me on "time-out" by having me stand in a corner of the dining room, facing the corner. Who knows how long I was in time-out, it felt like a lifetime, and I can't remember why I was put on time-out, but I probably deserved it. While I was standing there, I told myself, "When I grow up, I am going to be an architect and design round houses so no kid ever has to stand in a corner."

It wasn't until ten years later, in the eleventh grade, that I made the conscious choice to study architecture. Although it didn't feel like a decision at all, it felt more like a "knowing." I remember sitting in my bedroom the night before the first day back to school after winter break, and having an uneasy feeling about not knowing what I wanted to do with my life.

My other sister, Laura, had been gently pushing studying medicine and being a doctor, and I had been going along with that idea for most of my high school years, but that night it didn't feel right to me. I asked myself, "What do I want to study then? What do I want to be?" I honestly didn't know the answer and it was making me sad. Out of nowhere, I heard a voice, and I can't recall if it was from within me or outside of me, but it said, "You are going to study architecture and be an architect." That knowledge was so comforting and calming, the feelings of sadness and uneasiness went away.

Honestly, it was kind of spiritual. I shared that I wanted to be an architect with Martin, my oldest brother, and the following week, he scheduled a visit to the School of Architecture at University of Southern California to find out what things I could do while in high school to help me with my college applications. Who knew by putting me on time out, my sister had planted the seed, and my brother by taking me to visit a university with a school of architecture made it feel like a realistic goal. I graduated from USC with a bachelor's degree in architecture seven years later. My mentors and allies were hard at work even back then without knowing it.

In Summer of 1998, I had my bachelor's in hand and was working in architecture firms and was enjoying the work I was doing, but getting across the finish line to getting my architect's license was going to take me close to sixteen years to accomplish. I had so many mental blocks around pursuing my architect's license. I was dealing with imposter syndrome, having feelings of not belonging in the field that I was in or deserving of the income that I was earning. I had limiting beliefs that I was not good enough, smart enough, creative enough, just not enough. Attempting to pass and failing the licensing exams was only going to prove to myself that I was not enough and that I was indeed a fake.

For many years, I didn't even care about taking the exams to get licensed; I had talked myself out of wanting to get licensed. I told myself there was no point in getting licensed because I never planned to open my own firm, I was always going to be working under a licensed architect, and the work that I was doing as project manager did not require me to have a license. Why put myself out there, when I can remain small in my little protective bubble and avoid the risk being outed as a fake?

Throughout all these years of procrastination, I still had people in my life that would gently encourage me to take the exams. My family was there to support me at the pace I was going, never pushing me, just offering support and holding space for me. My close friend from university, Val for years, was always telling me, "Mony, you're the sun and everything revolves around you." At the time, I interpreted that to mean that I required other people's energy to exist and was self-involved. Now I realize that Val saw something in me that I still had not acknowledged or knew that existed in me. She saw my light even when I hadn't learned to shine it yet.

At my annual performance reviews, I came to expect the question from my bosses of where I was with my exams, and I'd tell them I was not ready or too busy, and they would nod their heads, but still would always insist that I take the exams anyways, that that there was nothing wrong if I didn't pass it, I'd just try again in six months.

Finally, at one point, my coworker and I agreed to team up as study buddies, be each other's support, motivate one another, and hold each other accountable to finally take the exams. That worked! I was finally able to get the written exams out of the way. My family, as always, was there for support and had my back.

My mom was the best. She would ask me when my next exam was scheduled for so she could *prender una veladora* for me that week; it became a ritual for us and part of my exam process. At the end of almost five years, the only exam left was the California Supplemental Exam (CSE).

Once again, I found myself stalling on taking that last one critical exam for a license in California. I was reluctant to study for it. I'd say I was going to start studying for it and I'd never get around to it.

Finally, things started to shift around me and for me. I had been working with a life coach for over a year. Working on myself, my self-confidence, and my self-forgiveness, I was able to clear out a lot of mental blocks I had been carrying around for a very long time. I also worked on letting go of the limiting beliefs I had about being an architect, that I was a fake, that I was not good enough. I finally got the level of growth that I accepted and acknowledged the strong, smart, confident, amazing woman that I've always been—the woman that people around me had been seeing all this time, but I could never see. I came out of my shell and was "shining my light," as they say. It brought out my confidence and increased my courage to take risks knowing that I would be okay. I stopped seeing the CSE exam as a huge mountain I had to summit, and saw it for what it actually is, which is just a method for the state of California to see if people answered enough questions correctly in order to issue licenses.

The realization that was the final shift of my thoughts happened while sitting in a conference room with my colleagues (2 partners and 3 other project managers besides myself), interviewing for a high-profile mixed-use transit-oriented development. I realized two things: I was the only person on our team that was not a licensed architect, and I was also the only person of color in that meeting. That was unacceptable.

I was limiting my potential of being the badass licensed Latina architect in a room. I owed it to my family, to my ancestors, to past generations, to future generations, to other Latinx girls that want to be architects, but most importantly I owed it to myself to take the final licensing exam and get over this irrational fear of not passing it. If I didn't pass the first time, I'd keep retaking the exam until I did pass the darn thing! So, I hunkered down and studied as much as I could. Two and a half months later, I passed the CSE and was a licensed architect. In the end, while I admit it was a lot of studying and the exam was not a breeze, what it wasn't was this huge monster that was going to kill my dreams of being an architect.

Thank you for taking the time to read about my life story and my journey with the licensing exams. If there is one thing to take away from my story it's this: Seek out the mentors and allies that are around you and ask them for support and advice. If you meet someone and they inspire you, take it as a sign that there is something about them that you admire and perhaps align with. Also, ask your mama or *abuelita* if they will light a veladora for you during your studying and exams, or you can always ask me, I will light a candle for you. Every person's path is different, and I support you in yours.

UNA COSITA MÁS

When anyone tells you, you can't something, prove them wrong. My freshman year at USC, a classmate advised me to change majors because architecture is a hard profession, "especially if your parents are not architects." That was all the motivation I needed. Here I am, a successful Latina architect working in Los Angeles inspiring other Latina girls to pursue their passions.

Do what makes you happy, let that be your guiding compass. Don't let the fear of failing keep you from going after what you want. If your energy intimidates people around you, that's on them, it's not for you to take on.

An excerpt of my favorite quote is powerful: "You playing small does not serve the world. There is nothing enlightened about shrinking so that other people won't feel insecure around you. We are all meant to shine, as children do. We were born to make manifest the glory of God that is within us. It's not just in some of us; it's in everyone. And as we let our own light shine, we unconsciously give other people permission to do the same. As we are liberated from our own fear, our presence automatically liberates others."—Marianne Williamson

BIOGRAPHY

Monica Rodriguez is a licensed architect from Los Angeles, CA. She knew she wanted to be an architect at a very young age; with perseverance, drive, and her family's support, she's never looked back. She is the proud daughter of two wonderful parents from Tepetongo, Zacatecas, Mexico, and a proud sister of four supportive older siblings, Leticia, Martin, Laura, and Carlos. Her passion projects are low-income, multi-family projects. As a second-generation Mexican-American and LA native, Monica likes volunteering her time at a number of organizations to encourage and inspire children to pursue their dreams and shine their light.

In 2011, she co-developed a sixth-grade architecture mentorship program for Para Los Niños Elementary in LA. In 2020, Monica helped kickstart the current Architecture Mentorship Program that she and coworkers currently have with the Santa Monica and Mar Vista Boys & Girls Club, in the hopes to inspire BIPOC kids to be LA's future architects. Community involvement is also important to Monica; she is the Board Architect of the Jefferson Park HPOZ. She enjoys exploring other forms of creative expression outside of work including pottery and stand-up comedy.

Monica Rodriguez, AIA
Email: 411monica@gmail.com
Phone: 213-215-4680
Instagram: @theemonicaroxx
Linkedin: www.linkedin.com/in/monica-rodriguez-architect/

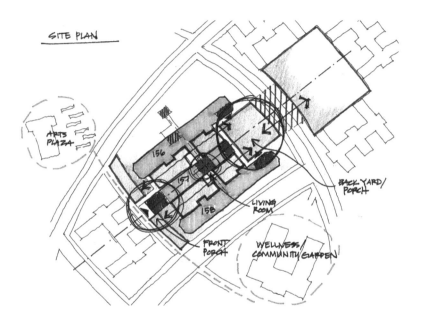

SITE PLAN

ARTS PLAZA

156

157

158

FRONT PORCH

LIVING ROOM

BACK YARD/ PORCH

WELLNESS/ COMMUNITY GARDEN

Partial site plan sketch for an affordable housing adaptive reuse project of three existing buildings in Los Angeles, CA on the West LA VA Campus.

Hand sketch by Monica Rodriguez

SIMPLY MEXICAN, SIMPLY AN ARCHITECT, SIMPLY ME

KATIA MCCLAIN

GROWING UP BLINDLY, WITH NO LABELS

I am Mexican. I was born in Mexico City, a very large cosmopolitan city, with beautiful hot thunderstorms during the summer, volcanoes with eleven-letter names that peak southeast to the urban metropolis, and a high elevation that can make winters a bit cold, making people constantly move inside of it.

This constant movement is like lightning bugs in a jar, and encounters seem to provoke people to know each other—and architecture is built around those social encounters. When I left Mexico in the 1990s, there were more than 80 million people in the city, many of whom were from other countries. To this day, the city is a mix of cultures reflected in our day to day lives. We eat tacos al pastor (my favorite taco) influenced by Lebanese immigrants in Mexico cooking the meat on a spit, similar to a lamb shawarma.

Most of the people in the city speak Spanish, but we have words from Nahuatl that we use all the time, like chocolate, avocado, tomato, and coyote. We love football (soccer) with traces from ancient China. We listen to Mariachi music, the quintessential Mexican folk ensemble, which has influences from Germany, France, and Africa. I was born in a mestizo culture: I can trace some of my family ancestry to Spain, and their migration to Mexico during the Franco regime in Spain, while also tracing my ancestry from my grandfather's side to the Mayans in the south of Mexico. I am not Spanish-Mexican or Mayan-Mexican, and for sure my favorite tacos are not Lebanese-Mexican. If you are born in Mexico, you are Mexican. Not French-Mexican, Zapotecan-Mexican, African-Mexican, Nicaraguan-Mexican. Simply Mexican.

In Mexico, while your nationality is typically asked in some government forms, there are no questions around the color of your skin, your ethnic background, your race, or where your family is from. In a sad way, the labels are less used because the people you know and typically interact with, are within the same circle and look like you.

The big divide in Mexico is around socioeconomic differences, and there are not a lot of socioeconomic differences in a large middle-class society like the one I grew up in. These differences are regional and are based on different dimensions from what we are used to in the U.S. In the U.S, the algorithm is defined around levels of education, employment, vehicles, and internet access. In Mexico, those dimensions are around healthcare access, infrastructure, connectivity, and education.

This is where my privilege comes from, a privilege that I took for granted for years, and for sure until I came to the U.S.

I enrolled in architecture school because my family pushed me to be an architect, and because it was a respectable profession for a woman. I wanted to be a marine biologist like the French oceanographer Jacques Cousteau. My circle of influence revolved around my middle-class family and friends. Then in 1994, the Mexican peso lost three zeros: if you had a thousand pesos in the bank one day, the next day you had only one single peso. My grandfather, who was the financial and emotional anchor of my family, never recovered after this; he fell ill and died years later of cancer. My family never recovered after that. I lost some friends, moved several times, and with the help of my grandmother, I reconnected with my father and my brothers who I had never met before. My life changed after that.

I was determined to not let my life change this drastically again. I had a chip on my shoulder and needed to get away from Mexico. I finished architecture school and defying conservative family traditions where family stays together, I managed to get a scholarship and travel around Europe for more than a few months. I was no longer living in the insulated society of middle-class Mexico.

After this trip, my days in Mexico were numbered. I had seen different ways of living life, so I decided to come to the U.S. and live with some friends. I arrived to San Francisco, California with about $100 dollars in cash, two pieces of luggage, an architecture degree, and my dreams to live a better life—a life where I could have a good job as an architect, with healthcare benefits, a life where I could be successful, be able to save money, and live a good life with friends and family. I didn't need my dream to be easy, but to be possible.

I HAD A LABEL: I WAS MEXICAN. AND IT WAS NOT A GOOD ONE

My first challenge was to find a job. I was determined to find a good job in architecture; I didn't want to do anything else. I was a licensed architect in Mexico, so it should have been easy, but it wasn't. Because my education was not from the U.S., my degree was not recognized, and I was not even able to call myself an architect—I felt like I had wasted five years of education.

The job interviews were the worst. I was told I was not going to get time off after lunch for a nap since "Mexicans are lazy and take naps all the time." I was asked if I designed always with "weird colors like Mexican architects do." I was shocked. I didn't know how to answer any of these questions; they didn't make any sense to me. I stayed quiet. After several interviews, I took a job with a self-proclaimed Mexican-American architect who didn't speak Spanish, and had never been to Mexico, but that was kind enough to give me the job I needed after a long search.

I knew and had read about California's distinct and very important connections with the outside world, so it was my expectation that I would be welcomed and recognized as a contributor to society since I had come here to work. That was not the case. With my native language being Spanish, I have an accent while speaking English. My writing uses the beloved passive voice in Spanish, corrected into an English active voice every single time, giving away my not being born in the U.S.

I was told that to be a successful architect, I had to network, so I did as such. After introducing myself in new circles, the first thing I am always asked is "where are you from?" after my answer, there is always a variety of follow up assertions by the questioning agent, ranging from "I love those Mexican sombreros," "I love Taco Bell" or "I am sorry" that perplexed me every single time.

I hated having to explain where I was from every single time. It made me feel like a stranger, never belonging, and it took me until 2016 and a presidential election to understand what the true image of Mexico in the U.S. is, an image that people thought they had to feel sorry for me for being Mexican. I immediately started taking diction classes, read books to improve my grammar and spelling, and tried to get rid of that accent that made me a foreign entity, a legal alien like Sting used to sing, and simply someone that didn't belong in the U.S. I wanted to belong, assimilate, and be like the rest.

In addition to the "I am sorry" the second comment that surprised me the most, at least at the beginning, was "you don't look Mexican." It was 2002, and I was at an architectural networking event. While going around the room meeting people, I was asked by a prominent Mexican-American architect in the Bay Area, "Are you Mexican?" before I could address the original question, there was one of those follow up statements, "You don't look Mexican!"

It took me a second to remember that under my business jacket, I was wearing a Mexico football jersey after the night before we had tied with Italy 1-1 during the World Cup in South Korea/Japan. Why would someone think that I wasn't born there? Why would they deny my existence? It was the light color of my skin that made me "not Mexican."

I was now facing a triple standard. I didn't belong in the community because of an accent, and I was discriminated because of it. At the same time, I was not Mexican enough because I didn't fit the mold that the world had created where Mexicans have a common skin color: brown. On top of this, I was alienated by those of Mexican origin in the U.S. with darker skin tones because of having a lighter skin.

I struggled for years to understand what to call myself in the architectural community. Was I a Mexican architect? A Mexican-American architect? Latina architect? Hispanic architect?

Race, ethnicity, and country of origin are terms inadvertently intermixed all the time. When I first got my membership with the AIA in the late 90s, I declined to state when asked about demographic information. It was a rebellious way for me to express my disappointment in the need to put people in boxes, fitting one category, when I am simply a human being trying to create spaces through architecture. At that point in my life, my identity was an obstacle that I had to overcome.

EMBRACING MY IDENTITY AND LETTING IT BECOME MY SUPERPOWER

I lasted almost fifteen years in my second job as an architect in the U.S. I was at a large firm in California, and I was in a meeting with a lot of white, middle-aged architects who were the principals of the firm. We were discussing a culture-shifting operational procedure related to salary analysis and benchmarking around gender and race; they all had the same opinion of not needing this extra procedure, except for me. It was at that moment that I realized the power of being different, the importance of my uniqueness, and the value of expressing that diverse opinion in a homogeneous group like the architecture profession is.

Up to that point, I had conformed to the rules, and I had not asked others to see what I was capable of or to give me or others a chance. I realized that I didn't have to overcome my identity; I had to embrace it. I was still young, and I was afraid that because English is not my first language, I would not be able to express what I was feeling clearly. I was scared of not belonging, but in what felt like an eternity, I gathered my thoughts, left some fears aside, expressed my opinion, and immediately left the room. I didn't wait to hear what they had to say. In retrospect, I wish I had stayed, but I was so afraid that I couldn't.

I didn't want them to change; I just wanted them to let me and others that didn't look like them in. I want to think I gained their respect by disagreeing with them and telling them why. At that moment, I used my voice and the label that I tried to fight so much to make a difference. I found myself and my why.

I am now a partner at a firm. I am the only Mexican and the only Latina in that group. I am the Chief People Officer and lead the culture group firm-wide by standing up, expressing my opinion, exposing labels and silos, and giving a platform to others that are yet about to find their voice. I am a board member of the Hispanic Foundation of Silicon Valley, where I have found similar voices facing similar labels empowering the lives of others in the community.

When people ask me now where I am from, I smile. I typically respond, "Where do you think I am from?" and it sparks an interesting conversation that I now take as a teaching moment to myself and to others. I no longer can stay silent about the importance of presence of diverse opinions in our architectural community. After more than twenty years in the U.S., I am multicultural and binational. I am proud of being born in Mexico, married to a Scottish-descended, super supportive husband, and practice as an architect in the U.S., shaping spaces and in a society where I can make a difference to others that are coming behind me.

UNA COSITA MÁS

It took me years and a lot of introspection to be happy with myself, my career, with my family, and with others. Being born in Mexico and a Latina in the U.S. is not an all-or-nothing for me. Labels create rigid binary solutions and ideas of success that set expectations that are not mine, they end up conveying something absolute, and I am far from being just one thing.

Find who you are quickly in your life. The sooner you know who you are, the sooner you can remove the labels that you have created in your head that prevent you from succeeding. Then you can be your true self and find your why. With your why, it becomes easier to focus on where you are going, what matters most in your life, and the decisions you must make to achieve your goals. The labels society puts on us shape our identity in the community and create assumptions and expectations that may be good for others but are not absolute. Defy this notion and define your own expectations, lean into you, obsessing over your self-created labels stops you from being an authentic version of you. You deserve to be here.

BIOGRAPHY

As a Steinberg Hart partner, Katia fuses her expertise leading complex, innovative, and highly sustainable projects with her passion for championing an inclusive, people-focused culture across the firm. Over the last three decades, Katia has worked to create powerful environments that have a positive impact on the diverse communities they serve. Her work expands from private clients and large mixed-use developments to affordable housing and educational spaces in higher education institutions that embrace a culture of inclusivity and diversity.

She serves on the board of the San Jose Downtown Association, the board of the Hispanic Foundation of Silicon Valley, and is a founding member of AIA Silicon Valley's Women in Architecture Committee. She is married to her husband Stephen and together with their dog Hunter, they love travelling the world, seeking new adventures, and learning about other cultures.

Katia McClain, AIA, NOMA, DBIA, LEED AP BD+C, LFA
kmcclain@steinberghart.com
408.394.6368 mobile

CASA BATLLÓ
ANTONI GAUDÍ I CORNET

Personal sketch during my time in Barcelona.

ON BEE-ING

PATRICIA ALGARA

I was born in the geographical center of Mexico. San Luis Potosi is a very traditional, colonial, and catholic city. It has many Spanish Baroque-style buildings, churches, and plazas; in fact, my grandfather, who was a renowned architect, restored many of them.

As a kid, I used to say I wanted to be a shaman when I grew up. I was not totally sure what that meant, but I knew it was a person who was connected to nature, to spirit, to plants and their healing, and who had a deep relationship with mother earth. I searched for books to understand how one becomes a shaman. That was before the Internet, and the library at my Catholic school had no books on the subject. When I finally found one, it said that shamans were male and born into a family that passed on the knowledge from father to son. I was so disappointed and mad at God—why would he make me the opposite sex of what I needed to be to fulfill my dream in this life?!

The knowledge passed down between men/from father to son in my family was not shamanism but architecture. Architecture is in my blood and my lineage—my father, grandfather, great uncle, and great-grandfather were all architects. As a kid, I spent time in my father's studio, drawing with circle templates and visiting construction sites. However, architecture also never felt like an option for me—like shamanism, it was a man's profession.

Unfortunately, as fate would have it, I was only exposed to it for a short part of my early childhood. My grandfather died when I was still a baby, and my parents separated when I was six years old. After that, I did not spend too much time with my father or his family. And then my father, like his own father, died very young of a heart attack. They did not live to see me become a landscape architect.

After my parents' separation, for the most part, I grew up with my mother and closer to her side of the family, which has some very macho personalities. Architecture, or any professional career, was not for women. According to them, a woman's place was in the kitchen, and education was unimportant. If a woman went to college, it was only to find a husband and become a mother.

Fortunately, my mother did not believe that; she was a single mother that worked hard to provide for us. She had her own business, and she believed in me. To this day, she is my greatest cheerleader—and she supported me in my pursuit of an education. I'm proud to say that I was the first person to graduate from college on my mother's side of the family, and I am the only one with a master's degree.

Although my mother's family was not college educated, I learned many essential things from them. My grandparents on my mother's side immigrated to the U.S. My grandfather worked hard and saved his money. His dream was to return to Mexico and buy a small farm in San Luis Potosi. I spent a lot of my childhood there with him. He taught me to douse for water wells, find the Huitlacoche mushrooms in the corn, and milk a cow. He instilled in me a love for nature, the soft feeling of the earth in my hands, and the intoxicating smell of the first rain as it touches the warm desert soil and the flavors of sun-ripened fruits. I like to think that my passion for creating edible landscapes comes from a blend of both of my grandfathers.

As I grew up, I wanted to study abroad and see other things. I felt oppressed by the macho and limited environment of my family and hometown. I got into college in Arizona, and I majored in Latin American Studies. I was not sure what I wanted to do, but it was easy for me to get A's in Spanish literature, theater, and film.

I was also passionate about the socio-political movements of Latin America and women's, immigrant, and indigenous rights. I wanted to do something to help other women to become educated and empowered.

I volunteered with a non-profit that helped immigrant women during my undergraduate time. After college, I started working at a women's rights foundation. We received proposals from all over the world, and I got to read them all. A common thread in those proposals was women struggling because of an environmental issue that polluted their lands and/or water and made them and their children sick. It got me thinking about how to address those issues, and what policies needed to change—who designs the spaces/landscapes these women live in, who makes these decisions?

Around that time, I went to the Latin American Encuentro Feminista in Costa Rica[1] and shared these thoughts with a prominent feminist. She said to me, "What we need is to get architects on board. They are the ones designing our cities." It clicked: Cities are unsafe for women because they are not designed with women and children in mind, because women do not design them. Public open spaces in the city need to be transformed and made safer for women, cleaner for the environment, and healthier for all. It got me thinking and excited about doing that, but it was not exactly traditional architecture, so I needed to do some researching.

I shared these thoughts and my excitement with a classmate from the Biosphere2, where I studied in Arizona for a semester. He said to me, "You should be a Landscape Architect."

Despite growing up among architects, I had never heard of landscape architecture. He told me his stepfather Pete was a landscape architect, and he invited me to his house to meet him.

---

[1] **The Latin American and Caribbean Feminist Encuentros** (Spanish: *Encuentros Feministas Latinoamericanas y del Caribe*) are a series conferences which began in 1981 to develop transnational networks within the region of Latin America and the Caribbean. The main focus of the conferences was to discuss and evaluate how women's marginalization and oppression could be eliminated given the existing economic and political systems by forming networks and strategies to create alternatives to existing norms.

He skipped mentioning that Peter Walker is one of the world's most renowned landscape architects. I knew nothing about him or the profession; I was so naïve, I asked him if he did backyard gardens. He was kind and invited me to his office to see his work so I could get a better idea. The minute I walked into his office; my mind was blown. I was so impressed by the scale of his work.

He took me out for lunch and patiently explained the differences in the master's programs at each university. I will never forget how patient, kind, and generous he was with his knowledge and time. That moment marked me in many ways. I was so impressed with the level of the work he was doing; I could see the profession was extremely broad, and that it was what I had been looking for. It was a profession that addressed the design of public open spaces through a community process and integrated the environment through a creative lens.

Without planning for it, I had found landscape architecture. Architecture had always been there, but the landscape element gave it a new light and a different meaning, and the emphasis on the plants and the living natural world was fascinating to me. Pete also showed me an important lesson in mentorship and making time to talk to people. You never know when your words and work can inspire and change someone's path.

Soon after, I got my master's in landscape architecture and started working at a design firm. I started an urban farm with a dear friend who is a permaculture master. This event coincided with the peak of bee colony collapse.

I kept dreaming about bees, and it seemed important to

have bees at the farm for pollination, although I did not know anything about them. I obtained a hive and started learning how to care for them. Over the years, my relationship with the bees deepened, and it has become one of the greatest loves of my life—and central to the design work I do in creating healthy habitats for pollinators and all bee-ings.

A few years after getting the bees, I had to have surgery to remove three large ovarian cysts. After the surgery, I was told that I had the worst kind of endometriosis (level IV), and that it had spread all over my reproductive system. I had been suffering with that very painful condition since I was 18 years old, without having it diagnosed.

I was told there was no medical cure for endometriosis, and that it would be impossible for me to have children naturally; a hysterectomy was recommended. It was a lot to process, so I went to sit with the bees to try to make sense of the news.

I shared my situation with them, as I do with any major news in my life, and I asked them to help me heal. During that visit with the bees, unlike ever before, I was stung maybe 40 or 50 times. It was an intense and painful few hours and I had a very strong reaction. I was covered in hives; I lost my vision and I purged everything out of my body.

I slept for about 14 hours after that and I woke up the next day feeling like a new person, full of energy—bee energy! I knew the bees had sacrificed their lives to offer their medicine for my healing. I knew it was a powerful healing and initiation I had gone through, but I did not know the extent of it at the time.

I have not had any pain since that happened, and I believe the apitherapy (bee venom) helped me heal.

Bees gave me a second chance at life, a life free of pain. That moment deepened my connection and commitment to bees. I read everything I could about bees and their healing. How they have been represented in the history of different ancient cultures, the mythology, the magic. I read about the ancient bee priestess of the Oracle of Delphi in Greece, the Mayan bee gods, and the sweet Melipona honey used for healing and ritual in ancient Mexico, and even way before that, the Mycenaean bee healers. Woman bee Shamans! I was beyond thrilled and wanted to learn everything I could about this.

The surgery and the bee venom initiation were very transformative in my life. I started my own landscape architecture firm because I wanted to do work that focused on creating healthy food production and habitat for bees. This is what they— and we—need, and this is what they were asking me to do.

Simultaneously, I dove deeply into researching endometriosis. I found out that endometriosis is a very common condition. One in five women in the U.S. have it, and it is caused from exposure to plastics and pesticides. I realized that the same pesticides that are killing the bees, which are the reproductive system of our planet, were also causing my infertility and pain. The same machismo and patriarchy that erased woman bee shamans from history and made me hate being a woman is also enslaving bees into an industrial agricultural system that is killing them, and us.

The path so far has not been clear nor straight, and there have been many unexpected turns. But I'm happy to know that I'm closer to my childhood dream than ever. I have a deep spiritual practice that is manifested in the world through the projects my firm creates with healthy gardens for all beings. The spaces we create are healing for those who experience them, but also they heal us in the process.

I'm proud to be leading a Latina-owned firm that has doubled in size during the pandemic. We are taking on projects with greater complexity and addressing issues of social and racial equity and climate change, but still we look at them from a spiritual and healing perspective. I'm proud of the work we are doing and how we do it; I'm proud of our diverse team and of our workspace, where everyone feels safe, respected, and challenged to grow. Everyone here can sing their song, lead with their heart, and embody their childhood dreams.

UNA COSITA MÁS

Today, I see that I'm finding a way to break through the male dichotomy and braid my grandfather's lineage with the lineage of women frame drummers and bee priestesses as well as indigenous knowledge and plant wisdom into my own version of landscape architecture that focuses on healing. In 2020, I got my license. I wanted to be taken seriously and speak about the importance of weaving ancient earth wisdom practices into our profession. Last year at the national ASLA conference, I gave a presentation about decolonizing the profession and looking into the wisdom of native ancient cultures of the Americas for inspiration. I opened the session honoring my lineages and singing a song for the bees into my frame drum. I like to think that I'm preparing the soil for the next generations of women to grow, blossom, and be empowered to incorporate healing wisdom into their creative expression of bee-ing.

BIOGRAPHY

Patricia Algara is president and founding principal of BASE Landscape Architecture Inc., a visionary award-winning firm in San Francisco and Portland. She is a recognized leader in coalition building and community-driven design. She creates landscapes that immerse children and families of all backgrounds and abilities in learning, exploration, and play.

Patricia was born in central Mexico and has always had a passion for empowering the most vulnerable populations by including them in the design of their spaces. She has engaged Spanish-speaking communities as collaborators in projects from master plans to urban agriculture initiatives, schools, and parks. Her community involvement and advocacy expand the boundaries of traditional landscape architecture.

Patricia earned a master's degree in landscape architecture from the University of California at Berkeley, and holds a bachelor's degree in Latin American studies from the University of Arizona. She studied the "Earth semester" at Columbia University, Biosphere 2.

Patricia has taught, lectured, and served as a guest juror at many universities nationally and internationally. She served as past adjunct professor at UC Berkeley and UCB extension. She has participated with the ASLA diversity summit and is part of the advisory board of the College of the Melissea, Center for Sacred Bee Keeping. She is co-chair of LatinX in Architecture SF.

She is the founder of With Honey in the Heart, a nonprofit that creates healthy habitats for and educates people about pollinators. She is the co-founder of the Algarden Demonstration Urban Farm, a center for permaculture education and natural beekeeping. She is a passionate advocate for quality and equity in the public realm.

Patricia has received national recognition for her design, outreach, education, and leadership work. She was the faculty advisor for two national ASLA student awards. A beekeeper and apitherapist, she draws inspiration from bees, whose artistry and industriousness demonstrate that beauty, function, structure, and communication can and should coexist sweetly.

Patricia Algara
Patricia@baselandscape.com
Phone: 415-509-3728
www.baselandscape.com
www.withhoneyintheheart.com

An early sketch of Mary's Garden at the Children's Museum of Sonoma County overlaying the metamorphosis story of Mary - la mariposa- and the Russian River watershed through playful exhibits and pollinator gardens.

KATHERINE AIDA SERRANO SOSA

A few things to remember (things I wish I could tell my seven-year-old self):

1. Every low is a lesson. Every high is a celebration and a steppingstone towards a new dream. You just need to figure out the path and what actions to take.

2. Everyone is resilient in their own way; don't let anyone tell you otherwise. All our life experiences are meant to shape us in one way or another. It is up to you to navigate and learn from them. Sometimes you will feel like drowning, other times like an easy swim. Then you'll get to those sweet moments when it will be like walking on water.

3. Your dreams are important. Develop a plan or list;

whatever that may mean for you and begin to act at your own pace. It's not a sprint, it's a marathon and it's not you vs someone else, but you vs the past self.

4. Believe in yourself, and your intuition.

5. Don't seek validation from others but from yourself.

6. Do what makes you happy even if it looks different from everyone else.

7. Stay kind, stay humble, and most of all stay true to yourself.

I was seven when my parents decided to move to the United States with me and my younger brother from El Salvador. To me it felt like an adventure, also, I feared the unknown: not knowing the language, and not knowing what my life would be like. Little did I know that one flight would lead to many hardships and lessons; yet, also, achievements and opportunities that I don't think I would have had back in El Salvador.

We arrived at JFK Airport on June 8th, 2000. It was the first time I had flown on a plane and the last for many years to come. When we arrived, we were lucky to have a place to stay at my uncle's apartment, but that meant seven people living in a one-bedroom apartment until my parents had enough money to be able to rent our own.

That situation itself didn't last long; sometimes family doesn't see eye to eye, and well, let's just say that before my family could have our own apartment, there was couch hopping between different homes. We got lucky to not be homeless thanks to the kindness of other immigrants. Living through this first chapter of my USA life, was life-changing, to say the least.

I'll be honest I was a pure brat before moving to the United States. I was used to getting my way, but it took little to no time for my seven-year-old self to begin to understand that life just isn't all sunshine and rainbows. I matured quite fast and began to comprehend at a very young age the social status, the value of a dollar, and so much more. What got me through it was the resilience I saw in my parents in trying their best to get my brother and me, and later my little sister, the best life they could give us.

By the time I was eleven, I had gone through my fair share of hardships and lessons that began to engrave resiliency in my essence. I was now an older sister to two, my brother was nine and my sister was two. At that age, I was their second mom, I took care of us when we weren't in school while my parents worked. My mom cleaned houses/offices, and my dad, at the time, was in construction. At times, my brother and I got to go visit the construction sites; it was then that my curious mind automatically fell in love with the idea of homes being built.

I eagerly wanted to help my dad and uncle, who at the time worked with my dad in construction, but because I was a girl, I was not allowed to. I only could watch, while my brother, though younger, was allowed to at least help pick up the trash and get small tools. I for one did not like that, but I kept being curious and would ask questions. One of them was, "How do you know how to build what you're building?" I was then told that they were building based on drawings that an architect had drawn and designed. Then it hit me, if I can't build it, then I will become the person who will tell them what to do: an ARCHITECT.

Looking back, I laugh because an architect does not directly tell them what to do and does so much more. Still, my eleven-year-old self began to construct this dream of being an architect, and from that moment on, I did not shift my sight from it. I did not really know how to prepare for it but made the best of the resources I had at hand, which was school and any research I could find online, to take action toward it.

My first step was taking a home and careers class in middle school, where we researched careers, we were interested in. I, of course, researched architecture. The research stated that architects were artistic, good at math, and designed buildings through the means of drafting different drawings that were used as guides to build homes and other buildings. From then on, I focused on doing my best in art and math classes. Lucky for me, math came easily to me. My mom from a very young age instilled in me that math was key as it can be understood in any language. Furthermore, she had told me that my education would be my inheritance, and it was up to me to take advantage of what was available to me to learn. It is something that to this day stays with me, as I constantly seek to learn more on things I am interested in, via any available source.

Through the rest of middle school, I focused on getting good grades and learning from the classes I was given. In my sophomore year in high school, I was lucky I was able to get a direct experience of architecture by taking the only drafting class my school provided. There, I learned the very basics of hand-drawing and even got to learn to use an ammonium blueprint machine to make duplicates of my drawings. The final project was to do plans, elevations, and a section of a home we designed. I loved setting up the paper, drawing straight lines, and visualizing a home in different angles and planes. This class reinforced my dream of becoming an architect.

Aside from that class and two art classes, I mainly focused on my core academics. I worked hard to get good grades, not only for what my mom had instilled in me, but because I knew that my college chances were lower than others. As an immigrant from El Salvador, I had and still have a TPS (Temporary Protection Status). In New York, this allowed me to get instate tuition, luckily, but I was not able to qualify for financial aid or for private loans; I would have needed a citizen to co-sign for me. Therefore, my only chance to be able to go to architecture school was scholarships because I had no college savings as we lived paycheck to paycheck. In addition, by the time I was ending my junior year, my parents had separated, and my mom was the sole bread winner of a household of four. I was diligent and focused even through this life-changing hardship of my family. In the end, my hard work of being in all honor classes and taking 10 Advanced Placement classes paid off as I graduated third in my class.

For college, I attended the William E. Macaulay Honors College at City College of New York. Having been accepted here meant a full tuition ride and benefits that aided my college career, such as getting a MacBook, and stipend for unpaid internships. This was a dream come true, especially since I also had a scholarship for four years that allowed me to dorm my first four years in school. I commuted on the last year.

The remaining expenses: part of my dorm, food, school materials, and travel, were still quite a bit of money, but with my summer job and my mom working seven days a week, I was able to graduate debt free, and for that, I am so grateful. My mom and siblings were the greatest support system during school. Not only did they go through a lot to help me pay through college but, also, for their emotional support that at the time I did not truly appreciate.

I wanted to become an architect so badly, yet that didn't mean that everything would come easy. I was so conditioned to be book smart that opening my creative conceptual side was hard. My first semester, I suffered. My study project wasn't conceptual enough, and unfortunately my professor and I did not coincide. I went into my second semester, honestly thinking I was going to change majors, but it took the right professor and even more drive from me to understand and embrace a new way of thinking, and for me to begin to blossom and feel more in-tune with my design projects.

From that semester forward, I saw myself begin to shift mentally in the way I saw the world and what I could create/design. Don't get me wrong; things were still tough trying to maintain a specific GPA to keep my scholarship, maintaining an honor student status and making time to go back home to help at home and be there for my family. Plus, I suffered from anxiety and depression, but my love/drive for design and architecture kept me afloat.

At the end of the day, everything fell into place. I went from being a shy, ineloquent student who was ripped apart during her first studio presentation, to owning my thesis project that received best thesis studio project. Five years flew by, and in May 2016, I graduated summa cum laude with a bachelor's degree in architecture, a research fellowship set for that summer, and a full-time job position at the firm I had interned the summer before fifth year and throughout my thesis year. Furthermore, I had my next major dream in sight, becoming a licensed Architect. During college, I had researched the steps to become a licensed Architect in New York; therefore, I had my NCARB account set up to log in my AXP hours and a to do list to get to my licensing destination.

Right after graduation, I did my research fellowship, where I got to take eight weeks to investigate biophilic design, a topic I had been curious about since I heavily leaned towards sustainability and passive design during school. During those eight weeks, I did studies, read various books, and developed an analysis of the topic. At the end of the program, I had developed a book with my findings and defining urban biophilic design. Once that was completed, I stepped into a full-time job where I began my port-graduate AXP experience.

I began my first full-time job at Notary Grupp Architects. It was a small firm which had no focus. Therefore, I was exposed to various types of projects, from schematic design to construction documents and evening learning to file with different building departments. I had been working less than six months when I decided to focus on my ARE exams; knowing it was going to be the hardest criteria towards my licensing. I began studying for my exams in February 2017, taking my first exam in April 2017. I happily passed and kept my focus on studying. I retracted myself from socializing and other things to do my best. The late nights and long hours of studying per exam worked out, because on December 29th, 2017, I took my last exam and had officially passed them all. Once I had completed my exams, I just focused on learning as much as I could at work and finishing up the 5,600 hours post-graduation New York state required to become licensed.

By the fall of 2018, I felt stuck at my job, and was having a minor identity crisis. It was then that I decided to look for other jobs with the advice and support of my family. Then in November 2018, I transitioned into working for Mascioni & Behrmann Architecture. There, I was on a new playing field. The company focuses on healthcare work; therefore, I had to learn new skills in developing the detailed sets that healthcare work entails. Also, I had to become familiar with the NYC code and FGI guidelines. I worked hard and in no time, I was managing my own projects.

What I liked most about the job was that I got hands-on experience with construction administration, something my previous job did not have, as well as learning more about various topics. It was here where I completed the final stretch of my AXP hours, I completed the remaining required forms and on September 23rd, 2019, I became a licensed architect. The moment I found out it was official; I became overwhelmed with happiness. I felt beyond grateful to have been resilient through everything I had been through and in making my dream come true of becoming a licensed Architect. Better yet, an immigrant and Latina licensed architect who could go out and make at least a small impact in someone's life through design.

Well, the resilient dreamer story doesn't just end there. At the end of 2020, I was going through another "stuck" moment and reevaluating myself as a whole. In the process of creating/evolving my identity, I knew that I needed to go off on my own and start building something meaningful for myself, and in April 2021, Rooted Architecture Studio PLLC was born. I publicly launched the company as a side hustle on July 1st, 2021. But on January 1st, 2022, I became a full-time employee of my company and a project manager consultant with M&B Architecture, as I slowly took the jump of being all on my own. Then on Feb. 1st, 2023, I took the training wheels off and now am fully focused on building and growing my company. This is the start of a new chapter as an architect-entrepreneur, and I look forward to seeing how it all unfolds in the years to come.

UNA COSITA MÁS

To be a licensed Latina architect means I'm one of the 1%... one of the minorities; yet, highly empowered to keep pushing boundaries and creating a new lane for others like me, like the amazing women in this book and others that came before us. I hope this makes path to many, many more Latina architects who keep pushing boundaries and making us known and making an impact even at the smallest scale.

Being a licensed Latina Architect and firm owner to me is being able to represent my culture, and provide my services to the Latino community, other minorities, and the public in general. Its being able to educate others on what is Architecture, what it takes to start and finish a construction project and so much more. It is making information more accessible in English and in Spanish. It is an ongoing learning experience that I hope never stops.

Lastly, being a licensed Latina Architect means being part of a supporting, hardworking, and loving community of inspirational women looking to elevate each other. Something I am proud of.

BIOGRAPHY

Katherine Aida Serrano Sosa is a NYS licensed architect who is native to El Salvador. Coming to the USA at the age of seven, she has set her roots in New York with a sense of respect and appreciation to her Salvadorean roots, as well.

Katherine graduated from the Spitzer School of Architecture in the Macaulay Honors College at CCNY in 2016, and in September of 2019 she became licensed in New York. With over eight years of work experience, she has worked on various types of projects at different scales and phases.

With her experience and knowledge, in 2021, she decided to create Rooted Architecture Studio as a gateway to help others understand the process of design and construction, as well as express her design language. To Katherine, design is spatial problem solving and each project is a resolution to the client's seen or unforeseen problems/needs.

Outside of Architecture, Katherine enjoys spending time with family and friends. She also enjoys being in nature and being active. She loves lifting and has participated in powerlifting competitions. She currently plays on an adult kickball league, and enjoys occasional indoor rock-climbing, hiking and skiing.

Katherine Aida Serrano Sosa, AIA, NCARB
katherine@rooted-architecture.studio
https://www.linkedin.com/in/katherineaserranososa
@rooted_architecture
rooted-architecture.studio

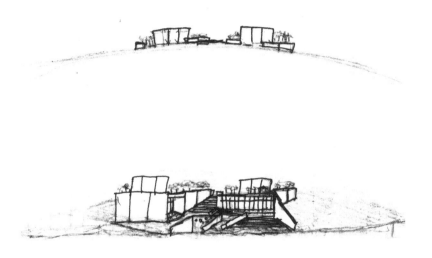

This sketch is from my Thesis Project design in 2016. To me it represents the passion I had/have for architecture and its relation to nature.

MY PATH TO BECOMING AN ARCHITECT

PATRICIA CENTENO

In retrospect, I became aware of architecture on the night of December 23, 1972, when I was six years old. An earthquake shook the city of Managua, Nicaragua, so intensely that it threw me and my brother off our beds. I have two vivid memories of that night. One is of my father yelling at me to let go of the *colchón* as he tried to carry me out of our room under one of his arms with my brother under the other. The other memory is of holding onto the mattress for dear life while my parents ran through the house over broken glass on the marble tile floor.

As the sun came up the next morning, my family and neighbors settled on an empty lot near our house, and we began to hear news of the devastation. Over 10,000 people lost their lives and some 250,000 lost their homes. By some miracle, we did not lose our home, although it had structural damage.

For the next six years, the devastation of the 1972 earthquake was part of my daily life. The city center was obliterated and never rebuilt. To visit my *abuelita* or go to the *mercado*, we drove around the fenced-off ruins of the city center.

My father's blue-print business was also destroyed during the earthquake. Like the *pinoleros* whose resourcefulness still shapes Managua, my father came upon a solution that changed my life while restarting his business. He built a structure in front of our house turning our living room into a blue-print shop.

As reconstruction went on, my father's business did well. Blueprints were always in high demand. Sometimes he ran 24-hour shifts to meet deadlines. Since there was no separation between the business and our home, I became a permanent member of the staff, who were mostly cousins. I loved helping during deadlines. The technology at the time was diazo white prints or blue-line process, which reproduced the original drawing. The paper came in rolls and was manually cut with a metal straight-edge ruler. I was not allowed to run the paper through the machine, but I became particularly good at slicing paper with the straight edge. I loved looking at the floor plans and pretending I understood them.

I was also vaguely aware of city planning and architecture through my mom's work. She was a secretary in the government department responsible for the reconstruction. Between my dad's business and my mom's work, I spent my childhood surrounded by adults talking about the daily headaches of planning, architecture, and construction.

Six years after the earthquake, Nicaragua experienced

another national calamity. This time political and, again, directly affecting my family. In 1979, the Sandinista revolution overthrew the government. Due to my family's ties to the ousted regime, we were forced to flee the country.

We arrived in San Francisco, California, with few possessions and little knowledge of the language or culture. Luckily, we had some family in the U.S. who were able to help us restart our lives.

I was a thirteen-year-old girl who did not speak English and had left my entire life behind: friends, school, home, clothes, toys. I do not remember speaking to anyone, outside of my family, for almost a year. Eventually I became comfortable speaking English, school got better, and I adjusted to the culture even making a few friends.

I discovered architecture for a second time in a high school drafting class and found I had a talent for it. Drafting classes were in the "shop" part of the school, where only boys took classes, but I loved it. My senior year, the instructor recommended me for an afterschool drafting job at a geology office. Unlike my classmates though, I did not understand there was a process to applying to college. A path to higher education was far outside of my immigrant family's experience.

I know that it hurt my mom that she could not help me figure it out. She worked hard to educate herself, and it was her dream for her children. When she was twelve years old, her parents sent her to secretarial school, because my *abuelito* said she was "the smart girl."

When I was little, she went to night school for a high school diploma while working all day as a secretary, and before we left Nicaragua, she had just started attending college. Even though I did not apply to a four-year university, my mom reminded me that no matter how I did it, I was going to college. *No sé cómo, pero sí puedes,* she said at the time.

I moved to Sacramento, worked at a retail store, and attended community college part-time for almost five years. During that time, I also got married. I was a twenty-two-year-old married woman, not sure about my path and feeling the pressure to have a baby, like all the young women in my family. While working at an art supply store, an architect customer suggested that I enroll in the architecture program at Cosumnes River Community College, and after two years, I applied to UC Berkeley.

Berkeley was challenging. I arrived as a third-year student, in a four-year program unprepared culturally and academically. Nothing I had done before could recreate the experience of a student who spent their first two years at UC Berkeley. I did not speak "architecture," the language, like other students did. The professors intimidated me, and I felt insecure about my drawing and critical thinking skills. I was a young married woman a few years older than most students, and I always felt out of place.

After a difficult first term, a few things started coming together. I realized that housing and community development were important to me. In Professor Sara Ishikawa's class, I fell in love with housing. Once again, a path opened for me. My time as an architecture student was too short, but luckily, I met a few mentors known for their work in equal rights, urban planning, and community development. Since then, housing has been my career.

I struggled finding work after graduating. I submitted resumes and sent copies of my not very good portfolio to firms for months without a response or interview. The pressure to have a baby was also a constant presence. I was the only one among my cousins who had not, but that was about to change. A year after graduating, my first son was born. At that point in my life, I do not think I had met a woman who did not have children in her 20s. It didn't cross my mind that I could have waited.

Nearing thirty, I still had not started my career and was not sure how to go about it. When I was feeling that maybe architecture was not going to be my path after all, I befriended a woman in my neighborhood in Oakland, whose daughter was the same age as my son. Her husband was an architect, and his firm needed help.

That encounter led to the real beginning of my career and a wonderful ten years at Van Meter Williams Pollack in San Francisco, a young, family-friendly firm. A year later, I had my second son, and I was able to take time off. Their focus was affordable housing and community design. I absorbed everything I could learn. I became good at assembling drawings, coordinating with consultants, detailing, and unexpectedly I became known as a "code guru." The wonderful mentorship I received led me to understand my role as a mentor.

One of the most impactful projects I worked on was Valencia Gardens in San Francisco, a deteriorated public housing project, plagued with high crime. Throughout the design phase, I was able to see how easily communities of color could feel disenfranchised, and how vulnerable the families must have felt not understanding the fate of their own homes. For the first time, I engaged with community members in Spanish, and I saw how important representation is when designing in immigrant communities. After community meetings, Latina residents, who would sit quietly in the back of the room, came up to me to ask questions they were inhibited to ask during the meeting.

In 2004, I met Ernesto Vazquez, a partner at MVE + Partners. Ernie was passionate about promoting Latinos and people of color in architecture. He was familiar to me. He enjoyed communicating in Spanish. He talked about recognizing and developing talent, Latino talent. I decided to work for Ernie and his firm.

He became a mentor and still is almost twenty years later. He often asked me what I wanted out of my career and what were my strengths and challenges. He encouraged me to think outside of the work I was doing day to day. I started to think that maybe I could become a partner in a firm one day.

The recession in 2008 was difficult for our industry, especially if you were working in multi-family housing, and for the third time in my career, I was searching for a new professional home. I was also facing the daily challenges of being a single mother, relying on friends and family for support, and somehow developing my career. I was worried about my ability to find work. During that time, my mom was my rock. Always reminding me, *no sé cómo, pero sí puedes.*

After a few weeks of submitting resumes, to my surprise, I received many callbacks for interviews. Even more surprising, I received calls from three firms over a weekend asking me to not accept another offer until I spoke with them! The path had unexpectedly broadened for me. In July 2008, I accepted an offer from BAR Architects & Interiors.

Self-doubt can be a powerful enemy. I had worked hard to overcome "deficiencies" I felt from my education, lack of cultural knowledge about art, music, and architecture, and lack of travel. I had become a good technical architect, but not an architect yet. I had good management and organizational skills. Why was I surprised that several firms wanted to hire me in the middle of a recession?

I spent two years at BAR feeling like an impostor, waiting for them to lay me off, while at the same time thriving in my work. Then I was offered an associate position. Within three years, I was managing one of the largest multi-family projects in the office, the most complicated and rewarding project of my career. I became one of the trusted managers among the principals.

I knew I wanted to be part of the leadership in an architecture firm. As I reflect on my professional path, I've always been teaching myself how to manage and was lucky to be working in a firm that opened those doors for me. Every year I would remember Ernie Vazquez's questions and plan my future.

After many years of giving all my energy to work and raising my boys, I struggled making room for licensure. I had taken a few tests, passed a couple, but then would fail one and give up. As time went on, I found that the tests I had passed had expired. I had to start over. The process had become demoralizing to me. But with the pressure of knowing that I could not get promoted without being licensed, I signed up for exams, attended group classes, and with a final determination, pushed passed all the ARE's. Then with a shaky sense that I had done everything that I could do to succeed, I took the California Supplemental Exam, and on June 6, 2016, I became a licensed architect. After the test, I sat in my car outside the exam center and called my mom to tell her I passed. I cried so hard I couldn't speak.

The next day, BAR offered me a senior associate position. Less than a year later, I was promoted to associate principal. In 2022, I was named principal. I am the first minority and Latina principal in the firm.

Since then, I have been involved in two organizations that help Latina professionals in architecture: Arquitina, a national organization committed to mentoring Latinas through to licensure, and AIASF Latinx in Architecture (LiA), dedicated to general professional development for Latinx. They embody powerful forms of mentoring and modeling that I believe in.

UNA COSITA MÁS

When I think back to the shy young woman who showed up during third-year studio at Berkeley's School of Environmental

Design completely unprepared, I know she couldn't see very far into the future. She could never imagine becoming the architect that I am today. She didn't know that, like many women, and more Latinas, she would spend her career over-preparing, worrying that she had to get it right, and having the sinking feeling that she always needed to know the answer, unreasonable as that is.

She may have daydreamed about calling herself "an architect," but she had no idea of how to get there. Sometimes my heart goes out to her when I think about her. But she had something that was as important as preparation and guidance to surmount the barriers. She had her mother reminding her, no se cómo, pero si puedes.

BIOGRAPHY

Patricia Centeno, AIA, LEED AP, NOMA, is a principal with BAR Architecture & Interiors, a 75-person architectural, interior design, and planning firm, with offices in San Francisco and Los Angeles, California. For Patricia, creation of multifamily and affordable housing has been the primary focus of her career for over twenty years.

A San Francisco based, licensed architect in California, she has been instrumental in helping successfully realize numerous award-winning housing communities throughout the San Francisco Bay Area that residents and the broader community embrace. A purposeful leader driven by team collaboration and integrated project management, Patricia has found that "bringing diverse voices to the table results in stronger, more inclusive and resilient design solutions."

She currently serves on the AIA San Francisco Board of Directors and is an AIA SF Latinx in Architecture (LiA) steering committee member. She is an Executive Board Member and mentor for Arquitina, helping raise the 1% of licensed Latina architects.

Patricia received her Bachelor of Art in architecture from the University of California, Berkeley.

She has two young adult sons, and when not focused on architecture, she enjoys reading, cooking, and spending time *con familia.*

Patricia Centeno, AIA, LEED AP, NOMA
pcenteno@bararch.com
415-293-7180
linkedin.com/in/patricia-centeno-aia-leed-ap-70a03317

People are going to live in and touch every surface in these units. Our goal is to get it right. The above studies represent four different ways to design 24 ft. x 30 ft. one-bedroom units. These quick studies show different kitchen layouts, various ways to enter the bedroom, closet variations, option to provide a study and an option to maximize living spaces at exterior wall, by locating the bedroom towards the back. Studying unit layouts is one of my passions.

EMMANUEL "MANNY" GARCIA

I've not traveled great distances in search of a better life in a faraway land. I did not struggle to have food to eat as a child. I was not forced to tend to a farm or store. I have not been judged for how I look to the degree others have, but I have my fair share of stories. I have not gone through these trials, because my parents, family, and others like them have done that for me already, and for that, I'll always be grateful.

My childhood was one full of homecooked meals, cousins' birthday parties, baptisms, Quinceañeras, volunteering at church, soccer tournaments, volleyball open gyms, yard work, vacations to Mexico, and the one time we went to Disney World, because my family valued family time, school, and service to others above all else.

After the joyous blur of childhood, I was privileged to be able to select what career I wanted, eventually landing on architecture by way of a summer transfer from electrical engineering. The little I knew of architecture came after helping with my family's endless home renovations. Opening up walls was fast and dirty, but closing them up forced me to think through things in a way I never did before. I figured architecture would be a good fit because I was always curious to understand how things were built since the times of Mr. Rogers' "Picture Picture" segments, and I had a love for art engrained in me after being inspired by my Uncles' graphic art careers where colored pencils, markers, and Exacto blades were always within reach.

I loved the architecture studio. I enjoyed the craft, the technical nature, and implied reverence that came with the profession, getting to learn a little bit about a lot of various trades and disciplines, dressing up for final presentations, the way in which projects are critiqued, the teamwork aspect of projects, the late nights, and the celebrations afterward.

Everyone has defining moments in their career, and my first came after a couple of years of drawing details of university buildings at my first full-time position. I learned a great deal, and my coworkers were all helpful and always willing to share advice, but I greatly missed discussions surrounding typology, historical context, designing spaces, and understanding the reason why design decisions were made.

This desire reached a point during a lunch and learn session meant to inspire the young members of our office. Our head design architect was going around the table asking, "What do you want to be doing in five years?" When it was my turn to answer, I naively but honestly answered, "I want your job." It was not meant out of disrespect. I genuinely just wanted to design spaces again, not just arrange details. He also answered honestly, "Well it may take you a little longer than five years, but if you stick with it, and make your way up the ladder, maybe one day you'll get that chance."

It was a simple boiler plate answer, but, at first, I took it as superficial jab, though, he probably thought nothing of it. Later that day, I realized that there was nothing wrong with his reply, and that the reason I was even upset was that I wasn't taking myself seriously. If I was craving a change, it was my responsibility to determine what I wanted and how to get there.

Not long after that lunch and learn, I reorganized my portfolio, entered a few design competitions, and joined volunteer organizations. People tend to notice when you're doing something right, and a few months later, I was starting a new job at Wheeler Kearns Architects in Chicago, where I've happily been since 2016.

However, even with a creative, supportive work environment, you tend to get a little restless after getting into a routine. For me, I'd found a job I enjoyed, great coworkers, and fulfilling project roles, but I was starting to realize that the projects I enjoy most are the ones where the space will be enjoyed by those who too-often are forced to make do with what they have at-hand. These are typically institutional projects where the new space is a result of community input and meant to improve the quality of life for everyone who visits. These are the projects that I realized I needed to specially request. These projects helped me refuel because their constraints aligned with a lot of the values that my parents instilled in me, creating spaces that will last and inspire while evaluating and prioritizing the building's needs and wants.

Around this time, I was also struggling with my own identity, my own Latinidad. Having been raised in a predominantly Mexican community, the experience of a majority white architecture program in both college and office environments was abrupt, but these were new, truly stimulating, and challenging, and I enjoyed it all thoroughly.

I didn't start missing my Latinidad until a few years after joining an office. My first few years on my own, sips of "canela," a few trips to the supermarket to host an "arrachera" at my apartment, and family parties helped me reconnect, but it wasn't until I was approached by my boss about a new project that I understood that I was lacking something deeper.

One afternoon, my boss, knowing that I was born and raised a Spanish-speaking Catholic, thought I should be given the opportunity to work on a new chapel renovation project for the Shrine of Our Lady of Guadalupe in Des Plaines, IL. I thought it was going to be a simple renovation, but quickly learned it would be extremely serendipitous for this to have come across my desk.

This project was unique in that the congregation was one of the few Catholic communities in the entire nation that was experiencing growth over the last few years. The reason for the growth required me to brush up on my own Spanish, Spanish colonial architecture, spirituality, and identity, all within the context of the Latin-American experience in the U.S. It's not every day that I get the opportunity to share this story with its deserved full context, so please indulge me.

Within Latin-American Catholicism, there is a tradition that exists called a "manda," or pledge, that is made to Our Lady of Guadalupe. It involves asking Our Lady to intercede on the faithful's behalf. Should the faithful's prayer be granted, that person is obliged to complete a spiritual pilgrimage to the Basilica of Our Lady of Guadalupe in Mexico City to honor their "manda." This journey serves as a humble way of giving thanks, resulting in millions of people visiting the Basilica every year. Unfortunately, whether it's due to poor health, financial hardship, immigration status, or the like, thousands of worshippers are unable to make the journey. As a result, these followers struggle with an unfulfilled spiritual obligation.

In June 1997, the rector of the Basilica of Guadalupe in Mexico, Msgr. Martínez, blessed and named the Shrine site the "Cerrito del Tepeyac de Chicago." As a result, this site was granted the faculty of being a place where pilgrims can fulfill their "mandas" to Our Lady of Guadalupe, as if they were being fulfilled at the Basilica of Mexico.

Consequently, the Shrine has experienced a continual rise in weekly worshippers and pilgrims visiting from the immigrant Latino community. In the late 1980s, locals established the Shrine with a grassroots effort on a 122-acre campus shared with Maryville Academy, a residential institution that has served children for over a century. However, after years of decorating and un-decorating a 1937 school gymnasium as a weekend worship space, Maryville Academy permanently ceded the facility to the Shrine.

The Latino community celebrates the Feast Day of Our Lady of Guadalupe annually on December 12th. In Mexico City, millions of worshippers fill the plaza and surrounding neighborhoods in a temperate climate for several days. In contrast, pilgrims traveling to Des Plaines endure freezing temperatures and heavy snow, which has failed to deter thousands of devotees that walk, bike, drive, and even ride on horseback in faithful groups from across the nation.

The year-round congregation at the Shrine recognized the extreme sacrifice that so many were offering to Our Lady. While holy images and a humble "cerrito" (a hillside meant to resemble the holy site in Mexico City) provided some sense of spiritual fulfillment, they recognized the need to have a permanent space of worship worthy of that sacrifice. Therefore, the congregation formed a building committee to repurpose the gymnasium into a chapel.

We were tasked with taking the building committee's various ideas and turning them into architecture, on time, and under-budget. This was not easy. Everyone had a different story they wanted to share, a personal experience that shaped them and their faith. Some of these experiences were profoundly intimate so it made the project very personal. Each of their stories deserved the time and space to be shared prior to us developing any schemes.

I'm inspired most by those who are willing to see past small differences to find innovative common ground. I say innovative because I believe that we are at our most brilliant when we challenge ourselves to do better, including myself. Everyone who was a part of those meetings contributed in some part to the final form and they were all ecstatic with the results.

During the pilgrimage in 2018, the Archdiocese of Chicago inaugurated the Chapel of St. Joseph as the Shrine's first year-round worship space. Our design team transformed the 1937 gymnasium into the Shrine's first climate-controlled, sacred space for over 6,000 weekly worshippers and over 300,000 pilgrims during December's annual Feast of Our Lady of Guadalupe celebration.

Construction crews reused over 75% of the former gymnasium structure, exposing the original timber roof deck and painting the original riveted steel trusses. A new glass and steel modern addition to the north, which inflects toward the Shrine, provides a fully accessible entry for visitors.

Like early churches in the New World, the sacred space is constructed with humble wood, metal, and clay materials. Side chapels, highlighted with gossamer canopies of wire mesh, warm wood paneling, and grazed with LED lighting, provide places of devotion for visitors of multiple cultures.

While dedicated to St. Joseph as a protector of the Virgin Mary, the chapel features saints from various cultures on each side chapel, reflecting an open invitation to pilgrims from all backgrounds.

Before the renovation, the parishioners casually referred to the space as "El Gym." However, after the inaugural mass that honored the fruits of their labor, they now refer to the space as the "La Capilla de San Jose."

The Shrine continues to grow, renovate, and adapt to its evolving congregation and I've been fortunate enough to grow with them as an architect and as a person. At some point in the project, we "hit a wall" where we were proposing something a bit too modern, in our opinion, when something a bit too traditional was preferred, and the reverend said, "Manny, these are all beautiful images, but if the parishioners cannot relate to them, then who is this serving?" This resonated with me deeply and I had to take a step back and make the decision to re-evaluate my priorities for this project. Our relationship continues to grow stronger and I'm happy to say that the Shrine has lots in store for the future.

The Dedication Service for the Chapel of St Joseph was one of a kind. The project was truly community-led, and to experience the congregation's joyful celebration in their new space was one of the most moving moments of my life. It wasn't until after the project was complete that I realized how many pieces had to fall into place for the chapel to be completed, and how different the outcome may have been had I not made the decision to reconnect with my Latinidad. This project inspired a visit to the Basilica in Mexico City, where my family and I were given a tour of the grounds and nearly a 500-year retelling, by a leader of the Instituto Superior de Estudios Gudalupanos.

In addition, this project also made me think that there should be more Latinx architects shaping the built environment for the growing percentage of the Latinx demographic in the U.S, because, if not us, who? This is why I currently serve as President of the Arquitectos Inc, representing Latinx architects across the nation to advocate on behalf of those eager for an opportunity. I was fortunate to have an employer who made the decision that a young Latinx architect should lead this high-profile project. There are plenty who would've said, "he's too young" or "that project's not going to be profitable," but they made that decision and for that opportunity, I am grateful.

I hope that this serves as a testament that you may not always know where the path of architecture may take you, but if you're willing to listen, have a good head on your shoulders, and a little faith, you'll end up exactly where you need to be and be all the richer for it.

UNA COSITA MÁS

Do not be afraid to act and be willing to bet on your own design intuition. You are where you are currently because you have put in the work. This is true whether you are doing poorly or well at school as well as in the office. You'll have setbacks, but, if you're proactive and trust the concept of delayed gratification, you'll realize or purposefully overcome those setbacks.

Being willing to bet on yourself includes trusting that your experience is just as valid as anyone else's. If you're Latinx, you're needed now more than ever. You are uniquely positioned to act as a bridge or translator between cultures at a time of great volatility. Your lived experience will become more and more important to the built environment as the next few decades unfold.

Take the time to understand where you come from, realize others are doing the same, and understand that your experiences may change over time. For me, the most exciting spaces and places are all the sweeter when you're able to share them.

BIOGRAPHY

Emmanuel graduated from the University of Illinois at Urbana-Champaign with a bachelor's degree in architectural studies and obtained a master's degree in architecture from the University of Illinois at Chicago.

Emmanuel has worked for Wheeler Kearns Architects since 2016, leading institutional, commercial, and educational projects including the Purple Llama Coffee & Record Shop, Ednovate's USC Hybrid High in Los Angeles, and the Chapel of St Joseph at the Shrine of Our Lady of Guadalupe in Des Plaines, IL—which has been awarded the Interfaith Design Award from Faith & Form and an Interior Architecture Award from AIA Chicago.

In 2021, Emmanuel helped transform a former bank building into a welcoming new headquarters for the North Lawndale Employment Network, a nonprofit on the West Side of Chicago whose clients include citizens returning from incarceration. NLEN was awarded The Driehaus Foundation Non-Profit Real Estate Development Award earlier in 2022.

Emmanuel is also an active leader in his community, serving as the current President for Arquitectos Inc. Most recently he has served as Biennial Committee Chair, AIA National Conference Chair, and Colectivos Chair.

Emmanuel is a registered architect in Illinois. He enjoys seeking out places where you can't hear the highway, playing soccer, and lives on Chicago's South Side.

Emmanuel Garcia

garcia.emmanuel.05@gmail.com

Quick sketch of my most rewarding project yet.
Conversion of a house into our casita.

THE PURSUIT OF ARCHITECTURE

ELIZABETH MORALES

As a child, I remember my mom talking about owning a restaurant, "La Chaparrita," she called it. I envisioned an adobe-style building; shortly after, it was on paper. All I knew was that I felt at peace with pencil and paper in hand. I drew my first two-point perspective at the age of eleven. My passion for designing spaces awoke before I even knew the word "architect" existed.

FOUNDATION

I began to envision the potential of spaces after my family and I started moving to temporary residences, constantly. I vividly remember getting home from school and seeing the things that were once a part of my very first own bedroom displayed on the front lawn. That created a deep feeling of loss in me. Following that night, I visualized what our forever home would look like if we ever had the opportunity to find a "home". To cope, I put my imagined home on paper as a floor plan titled, "My Dream Home". Drawing spaces began to feel like second nature to me.

During my junior year of high school, I took my first architectural drafting class. I was one of two girls and the only Latina in a room of about sixteen students. This would preface the lack of representation I would experience throughout my architecture career. Until this day, I cannot remember the name of the only other girl in my class, but I do remember that her bridge design withstood the most weight, and my design came in second place. I knew at that moment I was where I belonged. My foundation for becoming an architect began to be validated through hard work and perseverance.

Moments of adversity made me realize that the only option I had was to succeed. The older I became, the more aware I was of my mother's struggles to provide for my siblings and me. Our only option was to move forward. I have come to terms with life's hurdles and am grateful for the challenges I have experienced. They have shaped my mindset, and character, and enabled me to chip away at my fears and insecurities. As I share my journey, I would like to thank my mother for helping instill a work ethic, discipline, and resiliency in me. I quickly learned how important these principles would be throughout all aspects of my life, especially in my pursuit of architecture.

DETOUR

As I reached the end of my junior year of high school, I realized my GPA would keep me from being accepted to the architecture program at the University of Illinois-Champaign, my dream school. I remember visiting my older brother at U of I when he was completing his Bachelor of Science in architectural studies and walking through his studios, the scent of chipboard and sawdust filled the room. I observed models taller than me. I was mesmerized. When I received the denial letter after applying to the program, I knew that could not be the end of my dream. I took a slight detour, a different path with the same goal. I wanted to become an architect at all costs.

I enrolled at the College of Lake County, a community college near home. I was officially a college student. New textbook smells, fresh college-ruled notebooks, colored gel pens, and the hope of new opportunities stood before me. A part of me felt as if I would never reach the next step towards learning the architecture profession because there was no Architecture program at the college, and I was surrounded by people that would call it the "College of Last Chance". I needed to take it upon myself to take me where I wanted to be.

As the fall semester passed, I was craving more purpose than just taking my general education classes. Walking to class one day, I saw a flier with the words "Latino Alliance" reading across the top. I had never seen anything like it and little did I know this is where I would meet friends and mentors whom I would have for life. I was in awe; so many students looked like me. Not only in appearance but in the sense of wanting success and desire of helping others while achieving it.

During my spring 2010 semester, I was elected to be the

public relations officer for Latino Alliance. I believe this is where I found my voice. It was as if I let go of all my fears of failure.

Since starting at CLC, I went without architecture classes for far longer than I expected. Designing fliers for Latino Alliance allowed me to have exposure to graphic design, but I knew my desire to draw and design spaces was still alive and well. During my initial research of architecture schools, I slowly started learning about the licensure process. "I don't become an architect once I graduate?" I said to myself. This almost made me want to renounce my pursuit of architecture, but a good friend once told me, "If it were easy, everybody would do it."

Me puse las pilas, as we say, and I kept researching how to become an architect. I came across the abbreviation, NAAB, which stands for the National Architectural Accrediting Board. Their website lists schools that have acquired accreditation based on their curriculum. I was surprised that there was and still is only one accredited undergraduate program in Illinois.

My hopes of attending the Illinois Institute of Technology were high until I saw how much it would cost to attend. I asked myself again, "Is this a dead end?" I thought of all the obstacles I had already overcome and knew the only option was to keep pushing forward and succeed.

DEPARTURE

Determined to not give up, I widened the search, looking through the NAAB website in neighboring states, and found Iowa State University. And it was to my great surprise that tuition was affordable, followed by more options for grants and scholarships.

I was beginning my departure from my comfort zone and willing to leave all I knew. The idea of leaving my family was the most difficult. I came from a single-parent family and six siblings who were and are my best friends. Seeing my mother work from dawn until dusk and coming home with grease and metal shavings on her hands and clothes, I knew it was my duty to be the best self I could be. The sacrifice my parents made by leaving everything behind and immigrating from Mexico to give my siblings and me a better life stayed in my heart. I made my decision, and I applied to the School of Design at Iowa State University.

The day I received an envelope from ISU, my mom handed it to me and watched me slowly open it. At that moment I was overcome with the fear of rejection, but I knew that regardless of the outcome, I would find my way to architecture. When I read, "Congratulations!", tears of happiness rolled down my cheek. I was in disbelief, but I felt so proud of myself for honoring my family through my achievement. Holding the letter, my mom hugged me, and although she didn't want me to leave, she knew I had to seize this opportunity. This was one of the moments that affirmed my trust in the process.

The big day had finally arrived, move-in day! My mom and brothers drove me to my dorm and helped me set up. The departure did not resonate with me until I walked back into my dorm after saying goodbye to my family. I felt alone. I turned this pain into fuel and motivation to execute my mission of completing the architecture program.

The ISU five-year Bachelor of Architecture degree program requires all students to complete one year of their Core Design Program before being accepted to the architecture program. This added more pressure to my first year. As I began my design courses, I realized I had chosen the correct path. I enjoyed the assignments, which challenged my critical thinking skills and put my creativity to the test. There were moments where I began doubting myself. It brought back memories of the times I felt incompetent in my educational journey. I knew that if I wanted to succeed in the program, I had to rid myself of the fear of failure.

It gave me hope when I saw that my first studio professor was a woman and an architect. I had never met a female architect. She taught me what constructive criticism was and that **the process of creating something is just as beautiful as the outcome.**

ARRIVAL

A year after starting ISU, I received an email from the College of Design which would tell me if I had been accepted to the architecture program—and I was reluctant to open it. In the body, it read "Accepted." To this day, I can't find the words to describe the emotions I felt at that moment. I ran to my mom and showed her. In tears, I remember hugging her and jumping with joy. We shared tears of happiness, and in that moment, I knew her dreams of me having a better life had become a reality. Still, that was only the beginning.

In my first architecture studio, my professor bluntly told the entire class that we would most likely not find a job after graduation due to the Great Recession of 2009. Not what you would expect a professor to tell you on your first day of class. Looking back, I appreciate what he said on that first day. It fueled my motivation to not let that be my reality. As the semester progressed, I needed more income; who would have thought building a model out of chipboard would be so expensive?

Being eligible for a work-study position, I applied at the Greek Affairs office across the street from my dorm. Not being Greek, I felt foreign working there, but the convenience was unbeatable. I was the only Latina in the office until the president of a Latina-founded sorority, Sigma Lambda Gamma (ΣΛΓ), walked in. Our eyes grew with excitement when we first saw each other. I expressed interest in the organization and she invited me to lunch. To this day, I'm grateful for meeting a friendly face and *una hermana de por vida* who made me feel so welcomed in one of the most difficult moments in my life. Sigma Lambda Gamma was my new home away from home. The principles of the organization, Academics, Community Service, Cultural Awareness, Social Interaction, and Morals & Ethics added to my foundation of the pursuit of architecture.

As I arrived at my third year in the BArch program, we had our studio classes in the campus armory. The irony was that it was most likely the least aesthetically and climate-pleasing building on campus. I would roam the hallways and see army recruitment posters and the ROTC students practicing their drills. Since I was eighteen, I had wanted to enlist in the Army but I did not want to abandon my dream of becoming an architect. Once I was in the middle of my architectural degree, I felt like it was the right time to fulfill my duty to help those who could not help themselves. I had a strong enough foundation in architecture and I was determined to achieve both of my dreams. I enrolled in the Army Iowa National Guard. I spent my last summer of college completing Basic Combat Training (BCT) and Advanced Individual Training (AIT). During my last year at ISU, my weekends mainly consisted of studio work or attending army training, with the occasional socializing. It became difficult to juggle both architecture and the army at times. Throughout BCT and AIT, we recited the Soldier's Creed every day. The heart of the creed;

"…I will always place the mission first.
I will never accept defeat.
I will never quit…"

has been a way of life ever since. As difficult as it was juggling both architecture school and the army, I knew I had reached a milestone in success because of the love I felt for both.

Graduation was approaching quickly, and I still needed to find a job. I researched the firms that would be attending the Spring Career Fair and met with a firm that specialized in Department of Defense work. Coincidentally, the firm had designed the barracks I lived in during my summer at AIT. The firm offered me a full-time position where I began to learn, firsthand, the practice of architecture. I witnessed how trusting the process put everything in my life into place.

UNA COSITA MÁS

Throughout my pursuit of architecture and life itself, I have learned my strengths and weaknesses and have amplified them. **My strengths have taught me how to improve my skills and approach solutions. My weaknesses have taught me that I need to be willing to learn or unlearn things to become my best self.**

I am no longer a victim of imposter syndrome; I know I belong where I am, because I have earned it. I hope to inspire others to follow their dreams. Everyone should know they have the option to succeed. The process is as beautiful as the outcome. Trust it.

BIOGRAPHY

Elizabeth Morales, Assoc. AIA, is an Architectural Associate at BDE Architecture Inc. in their Chicago satellite office. The firm's headquarters is in San Francisco, California. BDE Architecture Inc. focuses on designing award-winning market rate and affordable multi-family, transit based and mixed-use projects while applying innovative site planning techniques. She has experience in retail, commercial, and Department of Defense design over the years. As an architectural associate and an Autodesk Certified Professional: Revit Architecture, she is determined to learning the evolving Building Information Modeling (BIM) in the profession to assist in producing quality and efficient drawings.

She is an Autodesk Revit Instructor at the College of Lake County and Waubonsee Community College in Illinois. She is dedicated to teaching architecture and BIM at the community college level to inspire students who are interested in the profession and build an awareness of the licensure process. Being an alumna of CLC, she feels a sense of duty to give back to the college by helping students navigate their options in pursuing architecture.

Elizabeth received her BArch with a minor in Sustainable Design from Iowa State University. While completing her BArch, she enrolled in the Army Iowa National Guard, where she recently retired as a Sergeant.

She is dedicated to learning the profession while sharing her knowledge with others. She hopes to inspire others to dream big even if that dream seems intangible, with perseverance one can go a long way.

Elizabeth Morales

moraleselic@gmail.com

https://www.linkedin.com/in/elizabeth-morales-5485756a/

A sketch from my time living in Rome.

RELEARNING MY NAME

PATRICIA ELENA ACEVEDO FUENTES

In the early summer of 2020, I was called to city hall along with five other community leaders. Amid the social justice movement reshaping communities across the country, we were convened to select a new fire chief and a new police chief.

The mayor referred to us in the *Rapid City Journal* as a "dream team." He said he had selected a "group which will be diverse in terms of race and gender – will consist of people who work here and know the city well and are respected in the community… They will be obvious picks – they are involved in the community, they're long-term residents." How did a brown woman, born and raised nearly 3,000 miles from Rapid City, end up on that dream team?

Ever since I left Puerto Rico to pursue a master's degree, I have been an outsider, first by being perceived (incorrectly) as a foreign student, then as a professionally-driven military spouse, and most recently as an architect in a profession, a community, and region dominated by white men.

Before I get too far, *"vamos a poner la mesa."* Let's set the table. I should introduce myself. My name is Patricia Elena Acevedo Fuentes. I go by Patri in the U.S.

Before the summer of 2021, I can't recall the last time I used my full name. After twenty-one years of living in the U.S., that summer was the first time a lot of my friends and colleagues heard that my full name includes two last names—and that neither of those names belong to my husband.

I stopped using my full last name when I moved to the mainland. First, because the woman behind the counter at the Florida DMV told me I couldn't have two last names - and I believed her. Second, I wanted to make life easier for my English-speaking friends. And to avoid having my name mispronounced, and to avoid having to correct others, and to avoid having to spell my name out every time. I wanted to get by and not feel like a burden.

I started using my full name again because I was selected as a Fellow by the Bush Foundation. The announcement would be widely shared on social media and traditional news outlets. For context and scale, the probability of being selected as a fellow is a 4% chance—or 1 out of 25 people who will be chosen—and in our case, twenty-four of more than 600 applicants.

A quote from Maria Hinojosa's book, *Once I Was You*, says it best: "In 1985, I was either going to fade into the background from trying too hard to fit in or I was going to shine as myself.

I decided to pronounce my name in Spanish. That was my authentic self."

After the fellowship selection announcement, I would no longer keep my head down and fade.

As a child of a colony who chose to move to the mainland, I have learned to be resilient: firm but flexible, adaptable, and accommodating. I realized that I have learned to assimilate in order to survive in foreign worlds. This is why most people didn't know that I'm not just Acevedo, but Acevedo Fuentes, and that my name isn't Patri, but Patricia.

I moved from Puerto Rico to the United States to pursue a master's degree in architecture from RPI (Rensselaer Polytechnic Institute) in Troy, NY. In architecture school, I was just one of three Puerto Ricans.

Until recently, I never thought about how hard I worked to fit in because I was foreign to my surroundings. Case in point, I even came up with a nickname for myself: Patri. I did this to avoid being called "Patrisha" because, the truth is, the English pronunciation of my name doesn't sound like my name at all. At twenty-four, I was dealing with seasons and snow for the first time, living in a foreign land, speaking a language that wasn't mine, and being alone. At a minimum, I needed to know when people were talking to me.

One of the other Puerto Ricans there, my dear friend Josh, told me he was so excited when he heard another Puerto Rican coming to the school of architecture that he cried. I think about that a lot. That was the last time for a very long time that I would spend time with someone like me.

My mom was a physical therapist and my dad was a pharmacist. So, for me to pick architecture, it seemed so exotic to them. We didn't know any architects or engineers. I chose a career field I had never seen anyone model. I didn't follow in anyone's footsteps. My dad would remind me often that my very first baby words were 'yo solita'—I alone.

After graduating from RPI, I alone went on.

I started my professional career in 1999, but it wasn't until 2005 that I worked alongside another female architect. I didn't meet another Puerto Rican female architect until 2019, after two decades of being in the profession. I spent two decades without someone who looked or sounded like me.

I have a rule I try to live by: if I want to complain, I have to participate.

So, after working exclusively under white male architects, under the unnecessary tense relationships with engineers and contractors, I realized I wanted a more collaborative and empathetic way to practice. I wanted to host a different environment, so I started AcV2 architecture in 2010, taking on the daunting task of creating a minority-woman-owned business in a white-male-dominated profession and region.

I quickly learned that if I wanted people to trust me with their projects, I had to let them know I was invested in the community. This is when I truly understood my sense of duty and found my passion for service. I made a name for myself by volunteering for organizations—starting small by serving on the building committee at our church, then being on different local advisory committees for the city on housing and downtown development concerns, and then asked to be on statewide nonprofit boards, and even co-leading the AIA Strategic Council. I assume that these are some of the reasons the mayor called on a Sunday, asking me to serve on his "dream team."

After years of continued growth and success, in 2016, I sold my company to a mid-size regional firm to continue growing and become a leader in a larger firm. And because nothing seems to change, and everything seems to stay the same, the sizeable regional firm I joined was 96% white.

I see a large part of what we do as architects as making data-driven decisions to create and affect the human experience. In other words, my job is to make observations based on data, then use those observations to make decisions and design experiences that will improve lives. So let me share some data here: There are roughly 110,000 architects in the U.S. While approximately one in five architects is a woman, less than one in 100 are Latin, meaning female Latin architects are less than one in 500.

What is the experience that this creates? I never had the opportunity to be mentored by or work alongside someone who looked or sounded like me. As someone who shared so little in common with my bosses and colleagues, my survival strategy hinged on taking every opportunity I saw. This is about making space for myself and those who come with me.

And then, in 2018, everything changed.

I lost both my parents between July and December. Being an orphan is like being unmoored; it is disorienting. I don't live in my country, I speak a foreign language, I don't have my parents, and no one here looks like me. How do I create a place of belonging?

Then I came across a quote I had seen many times before, but it finally made sense. In 1968, during the AIA National Convention, Whitney M. Young, a social worker and civil rights leader, delivered the keynote speech to a room full of architects. He said, "You are not a profession that has distinguished itself by your social and civic contributions to the cause of civil rights, and I am sure this has not come to you as any shock. You are most distinguished by your thunderous silence and your complete irrelevance."

That same summer, when I started using my name, George Floyd was murdered on a street, next to a sidewalk, in front of a store, in a neighborhood—that's architecture. Architecture is never just a backdrop. Many times, it's one of the main characters in history.

I'm forty-six years old… When I turned forty, I told friends that I was looking forward to my next decade of life, because I would stop giving weight to what others thought about me. By 2020, I was forty-four, so I had some years of practice being bold—and at some point, in 2020, being an orphan and feeling unmoored took the shape of freedom.

That freedom also pushed me to reflect on where I wanted to go and the work I wanted to do. And I no longer wanted to fade into the background. I also understood that the young women coming up behind me would never see me if I didn't stand up, the same way I hadn't seen another like me.

The Bush Fellowship selection was announced publicly on May 2021—and I was one of them. The morning after the announcement, I woke up to a message from the mayor asking me about my last name. His literal words were, "what is this Fuentes deal? I thought I knew you!" He was reacting to seeing my full name in print. To quote the musical "In the Heights," "Little details tell the world we are not invisible."

The Bush Fellowship announcement was the first time I had used my full last name (Acevedo Fuentes)—other than for legal reasons or to ease travel experiences. (Not surprisingly, airlines don't like it when the name on your ID doesn't match the name on your plane ticket. They also don't love it when you travel internationally without a checked bag, but that's a story for another day...)

A few weeks after the fellowship selection announcement, I was facilitating a discussion at work with a client team. The client was a Native American organization doing challenging and sensitive work around their truth. I wanted to show my authentic self to convey that it was safe to bring their authentic selves. When I introduced myself, I used my full name with the correct pronunciation.

That summer, our company hired a young Puerto Rican interior design intern—and she had been assigned to be part of my project team and was present at that meeting. She messaged me after the meeting, saying: "I wanted to mention that you using both of your last names and even mentioning Puerto Rico a couple of times, made me realize that I don't have to be afraid of using both of my last names, and to be proud of my background and use it as a tool for future experiences."

Immediately after that meeting, she started using her full name and taught the IT team to type accents on the keyboard. Angélica graduated in May 2021, and it took her less than a month to use her full name. It took me twenty-one years.

It wasn't that in those twenty-one years I felt like an impostor. It was that I was always the odd one out. I didn't belong not because I was underqualified. I didn't belong because no one else looked like me. Like that Sesame Street song, *'una de estas cosas no es como las otras, una de estas cosas no es igual.'* One of these things is not like the other.

While it took me twenty-one years to use my full name, it took me twenty-two to realize that it's not that I don't fit into the traditional practice of architecture, but rather that traditional architecture doesn't fit me. Again, I alone went on to design a different future for myself.

Who are we not seeing? Who do our actions affect that we have no idea are watching? Who are we leaving behind? I am here to make space – for myself and those who come with me.

UNA COSITA MÁS

Going back to that rule that says if I want to complain, I have to participate. To me it means that before I complain about something if I can change whatever it is for the better, I must try. For many years I heard a quote that says something like "if you're not at the table, you're on the menu." Many of us – women, people of color, those of us with accents, of different ability levels, of different socioeconomic status – don't have a seat at that table. That seating chart was made to exclude us. But one day I heard a quote from Shirley Chisholm, the first Black woman to be elected to the U.S. Congress, that said "If they don't give you a seat at the table, bring a folding chair." That's what I wake up every day hoping to do – to make this world better either by designing or advocating for more inclusive and kinder solutions. Making space for me and others like me. So, if you find yourself daydreaming about a world (no matter how big or small) that fits you, that represents you, that makes you feel welcome and safe, then you should go after it. We need more people like you.

BIOGRAPHY

Patricia is passionate about creating an equitable approach to community and design. She understands that architecture is powerful and permanent. As an architect, she seeks to make the design and construction of places and spaces more inclusive.

She brings over twenty years of design expertise, cultural sensitivity, and a wild and wonderful wit to her work. Born and raised in San Juan, Puerto Rico, Patricia resided in New York, Florida, and Texas before making the Black Hills her home. She finds joy in adaptively reusing existing buildings and creating infill solutions that catalyze smart growth and renewal with a special love for rural and remote communities.

An engaged and passionate civic leader, Patricia is a 2021 Bush Foundation Fellow. During the fellowship, she is expanding her knowledge of public policy and social justice and her capacity for intercultural development to create a more equitable approach to architecture through policy, planning, practice, and participation.

Patricia Elena Acevedo Fuentes, AIA, NCI CS
Patri.acevedo.fuentes@gmail.com
IG and Twi: @patri_acv2

IMMIGRANTS, MIGRANTS, AND THE DREAM TO BECOME AN ARCHITECT

DANIEL PEREZ

My family story is the story of immigrants, migrants, and dreams. My father was born in San Francisco del Mezquital, Durango, Mexico, and my mother was born in Crystal City, Texas. My father was born in the aftermath of the Mexican Revolution. His father was killed when he was an infant and his mother raised him and a sister.

He assumed the position of "the man of the house" at a very early age, and attended school up to the second grade. My mother was the youngest of seven children and attended school up to fourth grade. My father started coming to the U.S. at the age of eighteen under the Bracero Program, while my mother's family would work seasonally doing agricultural work in various parts of the U.S.

She and my father met in Montana in the mid-1950s

while doing agricultural work. They corresponded for four years before getting married. They initially lived in Arizona. My dad was deported just before my eldest sister was born and separated from his young family for months. With the help of the Mexican Consul in Phoenix and a judge in Texas, my dad was able to establish permanent residency and rejoin my mom and infant sister. They then moved to Idaho. My parents placed great importance on education. They wanted to give their children the opportunity they were not afforded.

I was born and raised in southeastern Idaho, on the outskirts of a small rural town called Rupert. I have four sisters, three older and one younger. Like many kids raised in rural America, my sisters and I started working summers once we were in junior high. We worked in the fields thinning sugar beets and weeding potatoes. Our parents wanted us to learn the value of work and money. I got my first in-town job at a grocery store when I was fourteen years old and obtained my first driver's license.

Throughout my youth, I had an interest in architecture. I knew I wanted to be an architect when I was seven years old. My exposure to what an architect did, at the time, was Mike Brady of the Brady Bunch at his drafting table and the short-lived experience of working for the eccentric client Beebe Gallini. I would draw floor plans and elevations of houses and give them to some of my sister's girlfriends that I had crushes on.

My parents briefly moved the family to Illinois when I was ten years old. Some cousins took us to the John Deere Headquarters in Moline, Illinois. I didn't know who Eero

Saarinen was at the time, but I knew I was experiencing architecture. It was settled; I would pursue architecture as a career. After living a few months in East Moline and Van Wert, my parents decided to move the family back home to Rupert.

My father was very industrious and decided to expand our home. He drew the plans himself, acted as the general contractor, and enlisted friends and family in the construction of the project. He had friends that helped to install the foundation, framing, and exterior sheathing. My mom, sisters, and I helped lay the exterior siding and gypsum board interior.

On a chilly day in early November, the signs of a snowstorm appeared on the horizon. I was on the roof with my dad helping him lay plywood over the roof framing so that roof felt and shingles could get installed.

My mom was also very industrious. She worked full-time, cooked, cleaned, raised five children, was an Avon Lady, and sold Tupperware and jewelry. My mom was hosting a Tupperware party with several ladies attending while my dad and I were installing the roof sheathing.

My dad went to grab a sheet of plywood that started to slide down the roof gable. He slipped and ended up falling between the roof rafters and ceiling joists, and landed on the plywood subfloor of the future dining room. I raced off the roof to find a group of ladies screaming while my dad lay on the subfloor and was struggling to breathe. He broke six ribs and punctured a lung, which explained why he was turning blue.

My dad ended up at the hospital for a lengthy stay. A group

of my parents' friends rallied to complete the roof installation before the winter storms arrived. There were many lessons I learned on this day, and am reminded of them every time I recount this story. I think about entrepreneurship, community, audacity, gumption, and how this was my earliest experience of the construction process. Nowadays, I also think about how I recommend people hire an architect when undertaking a home remodel or addition.

I took a drafting class in my senior year of high school and applied to the architecture program at the University of Idaho in Moscow. I was accepted with a partial scholarship.

I made the 700-mile drive to northern Idaho, and all four of my wisdom teeth had come in. I arrived in Moscow, my mouth was in severe pain, and I thought it is really beautiful here but I need to go somewhere else. I called my mom and dad to tell them I was coming home. I went to see the dentist and took a year off. I worked at a potato processing factory in the graveyard shift for a year and I was able to save money for college. This experience served as added incentive to pursue my dream of studying to become an architect.

Three of my sisters went to trade schools. Another sister and I ended up going to a university for our undergraduate degrees. My parents were very supportive, and they sacrificed so much to help me and my sisters. It was especially difficult for them having two children attending college at the same time.

After my unplanned gap year, I was accepted to the architecture program at Arizona State University in Tempe. The program was set up for students to take a list of required classes for two years in a lower division program, and then apply to the upper division professional program. Fifty students were accepted per year in the competitive professional program. I didn't get in the first time I applied, but I was encouraged by an African American professor, Rushia Fellows, to keep persevering.

I took an additional year of courses in art and architectural history, cultural geography, and anthropology, and worked on improving my portfolio. I reapplied to the professional program and was accepted.

My first design studio instructor advised me to think of a way to practice architecture out of design. I decided to ignore her advice. Professor Fellows was the only person of color on the faculty of ASU CED at the time, and there were only three Latinx students in my graduating class. I earned my Bachelor of Science in design in architectural studies.

I took an architecture and urban design summer course in Italy after graduation. The class traveled to Venice, Verona, Florence, and Rome. I traveled through Europe with a friend after the class ended. The experience of traveling to major urban centers like Paris, Barcelona, Rome, Athens, Vienna, and Munich made me decide that I needed to live in a large urban center. I set my sights on the largest city in the U.S., and moved to New York City.

New York was very different from where I grew up and went to college, and that was part of the City's appeal. I decided I should work at a variety of offices to figure out what resonated for me. I did the S, M, and L office exploration but not necessarily in that order. My first job at Gerald Allen and Associates was at a small firm with residential and church projects. I then worked at HOK with a team on a general aviation terminal and cargo facility for Japan Airlines at JFK International Airport. My last job in NYC was at Eisenman Architects, where I had a six-month stint working on the Columbus Convention Center and the DAAP-University of Cincinnati.

I discovered that I preferred working at small and medium-sized offices best because I got to wear different hats. Working and living in NYC was both exciting and challenging. I loved the idea that on any given day, I could go visit a famous painting or see a play on Broadway, but there were also the harsh realities of living on a junior designer's salary in a very expensive city. New York City made me become more assertive because it is not an easy place to live. I would still recommend for a young person to live in NYC at least once in their life.

When I left college, I made the commitment to myself that I would work for three years and then apply to graduate school. My undergraduate degree required that I pursue a master of architecture program to become licensed. I applied to the University of Illinois Chicago and UC Berkeley. I was accepted to both programs. Peter Eisenman advised I should go to UIC, but ultimately, I chose Berkeley. Coming back to the West gave me the chance to be geographically closer to my family in Idaho. I completed my master of architecture degree in 1993. I was the first person in my family to obtain a graduate degree. This was a huge achievement and milestone for my family and me.

After graduation from Berkeley, I worked for small and medium-sized firms in the Bay Area. Working at small and medium-sized firms gave me the opportunity to wear a lot of different hats where I gained experience in all project phases including marketing, interviewing, and reviewing contracts.

I worked with the firm Del Campo & Maru for a little over three years. Martin Del Campo was a true gentleman and a great mentor. He always had a smile on his face and a sparkle in his eye for life and the architectural profession. He had amazing stories of his family's migration from Europe to Mexico, and his migration to the U.S.

I worked on the Chicano/ Mexican American Cultural Center in San Jose, CA. I didn't realize at the time what a fantastic opportunity this project was for my career. It was an opportunity to work with and serve communities that look like me. I also had the opportunity to work on a project in Manila, Philippines in 1994, and met people that I am still friends with to this day. The project was rehabilitating an existing building into facilities for Epson and Iomega companies. Before returning to the U.S., I traveled to Hong Kong, Nepal, Tibet, Bangkok, and Cambodia. This was a fantastic education for me culturally and architecturally. I appreciated Martin and remained friends with him until he passed away in 2007.

I started taking the architectural licensing exams in 1995, and became licensed in 2000. At the time, the exams were offered twice a year in person. There were nine exam sections offered over a three-day period. I passed five sections in my first sitting. It then took me four years to complete the remaining sections and a final oral examination.

The design exam was a twelve-hour session and candidates were required to bring a mini-drafting board, and drafting tools, and pack a lunch. On my second try to pass this exam, I went to eat at a Taco Bell and had a PowerBar the night before, and ended up with food poisoning. The following morning, I proceeded to take the design exam, and had my drafting board, but forgot all my drafting tools.

I went to an exam proctor and explained my dilemma. She was very nice and asked other exam candidates nearby if they could lend drafting tools. Fellow examinees were kind and lent me the necessary tools. The lead proctor announced that when the time was called, pencils needed to be put down, and if this instruction wasn't followed the candidate could be disqualified. The twelve hours passed quickly and time was called.

I heard a loud voice screaming, "Put that pencil down, you are disqualified." I looked in my hand to see if I was holding a pencil, and thank goodness I wasn't. It was the nice proctor yelling and the disqualified candidate was sitting next to me.

In 1997, ARE testing was computerized. I eventually passed the balance of the written exams. The oral exam was my final hurdle. It was a bizarre setup in a hotel room with three examiners behind a table and a bed behind them. They would take turns asking questions. It took me three times to pass this exam, but I finally did it.

I started my firm, Studio Perez, in 2005. With my diverse

work experience, I had the confidence, with a little bit of naiveté, to start my company. I have now operated my firm for 16 years. My work includes a diverse portfolio of K-12 education, affordable multi-family housing, public work, and commercial projects. My interest has grown to serve underrepresented communities whenever possible.

UNA COSITA MÁS

Participation and representation are very important to me, as an architect and a Latino. I joined the American Institute of Architects to promote my architectural profession and community. One of my colleagues used to say, "If you don't toot your own horn, nobody is going to toot it for you." This is incredibly true.

I have realized the importance of activism and advocacy. I spent much of my career thinking, where are my people? It finally occurred to me that I could play an active role in recruiting Latinx youth to the profession, and mentoring emerging professionals. I became active with the AIA SF Mentorship Committee in 2009, eventually becoming Chair in 2015. I currently serve on the AIASF Latinx in Architecture Steering Committee to develop programming that amplifies the voices of LatinX designers. There is more work to be done in removing the barriers for Latinx students into the architectural profession.

I have had my challenges and successes in my trajectory of becoming an architect. The message I hope to send to Latinx youth is *"si se puede."* Do not let anyone who tells you that you can't be or do something define you. Celebrate your successes and embrace and learn from your mistakes and failures. Never give up on your dreams.

BIOGRAPHY

Daniel Perez founded Studio Perez, a San Francisco, California-based design firm in 2005, practicing architecture, interior design, and master planning in Northern California. The majority of his thirty years of professional experience have been on public projects ranging from education, convention, and cultural centers, transportation facilities, affordable multi-family housing, and a wide variety of commercial projects. He advocates for sustainable principles to design energy-efficient buildings that tread lightly on the environment and promote the health and well-being of building occupants. Daniel is a proponent of justice, equity, diversity, and inclusion in the architectural profession and the built environment.

Studio Perez is a mission-driven practice invested in helping communities and organizations achieve their goals. Many of the projects undertaken in the studio focus on serving underrepresented communities. Current representative projects include the rehabilitation of three existing buildings. The Digital Arts and Culinary Academy project in East Oakland provides learning opportunities for minority youth. The Mission Cultural Center for Latino Arts in San Francisco provides classes, performances, and programming for the Latinx community. 1005 Powell is a 65-unit residential SRO building in SF Chinatown that will preserve affordable housing for the Chinese community.

Daniel has served on the AIA San Francisco Board since 2016 and is currently serving as 2023 President.

Daniel Perez, AIA, NOMA, LEED AP

dperez@studioperez.com

415-503-0329

LinkedIn:https://www.linkedin.com/in/daniel-perez-213779a/

Twitter: @Zerepnad

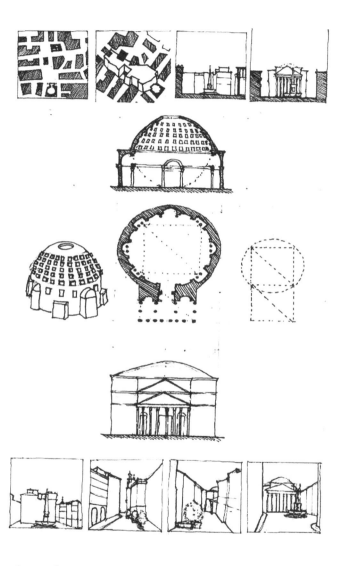

The sketches are from a summer class 'Architettura Italia, Analytical Techniques of Architectural Drawing, Elements of Historic Urbanism'.

VERONICA POCHET

What other career can you work at into your 80s if you want and enjoy each day solving different problems? Architecture brings together the best aspects of design, project management, and community building. I hope everyone can find a career that can provide them the professional fulfillment, financial security, and personal satisfaction that I have found. Architecture is a great profession.

I work in a small firm and I get to do a little bit of everything. Before designing a building, I get to engage forward-looking owners with a vision for a future building. The delicate alignment of hopes, budget, and public safety can be frustrating, exhausting, and always exhilarating.

Once we have an overall requirement for a building, we can start putting plans together. Besides the stereotypical work people expect architects to do like figuring out how many stairways are needed and drafting plans, coordination among an ever-growing cadre of domain experts is a key aspect of my job. I spend my day working across all disciplines including structural and electrical engineers, plumbing, and environmental experts. Each specialty can meet the needs of the building, but making each group's solution work with the overall building is my job.

Keeping forward progress with each stakeholder focused on their small part always makes me remember the story of the blind men describing different parts of an elephant. Often the domain experts don't share a common vocabulary, leaving architects to be the translators. I can go from a meeting with structural engineers to move support columns in a drawing to a construction site where they need a speedy solution to unexpected soil conditions. When working with our heterogeneous team of different educations and backgrounds, we collaborate and explore different solutions each day solving big and small problems.

How you grow up influences the way you come up with solutions, how you view people, and how you look at the world. I was eight when I came to the U.S. from war-torn El Salvador. Despite surviving an earthquake and living through civil war, my childhood memories of El Salvador are mostly made up of the good times.

One of my earliest memories is dressing up in indigenous clothing during the *Virgen de Guadalupe* feast day at the Basilica of Guadalupe. My mom would gather all of us and we would make the long trek from our *colonia,* our neighborhood, to the basilica. I didn't know it then, but the joy and feeling of community that the plaza in front of the basilica brought everyone would set me down a path of community-focused architecture. We would spend time in the busy plaza where vendors congregated selling food, candy, and relics and looking up to see the grand structure of the Spanish baroque basilica. I remember entering the building and being enthralled by the massive volume of the nave and the black-and-white pattern of floor tile. The yellow tones and the glass stained windows illuminated the space. It was probably the most beautiful building I had seen in my whole childhood. And I can never separate the beauty of the building from the joy of the community in and around that building.

The best feeling in the world is walking into a finished project and knowing that I had a hand in making it happen. The best projects are the ones that also offer a new space that becomes part of the community.

Problem-solving in architecture is my passion, but I would not be successful at it without the love and support of my family. My family came to this country like many immigrants looking for a better life. When I first started school in America, bullies made fun of me for not knowing English. I cried and went to my mom for help. My mom looked at me and smiled and said, "Veronica, don't let anyone define who you are. Remember that you are special and you can do anything you set your mind to."

That first year I worked hard, and studied English in every way possible. My whole family helped whenever and however they could. After my first year at school in my new country, I learned enough English to move to advanced classes and didn't have to be around the bullies anymore. That set a pattern for the rest of my life. Work hard, accept all the help offered by family, friends, and my community, and keep moving forward.

At school, having started in the ESL (English as a Second Language) path, I was not placed on a college-bound/gifted track. I fought to be in gifted classes, my family helped me prove I could move to the college track with every test and every homework assignment. Eventually, I achieved my goal of a college track schedule in high school.

None of my siblings were able to go to college. They were smart but they had many obstacles that made it impossible for them to attend. As the baby of the family, I had the benefit of time—time to move to a college track in high school, time to learn English without the pressure of providing financial support to the family, and time to dream.

The timing proved even more important as high school graduation approached. After years of paperwork and interviews, I became a resident a month before high school graduation. Residency brought the opportunity for scholarships and an easier path to college acceptance. My acceptance into Virginia Tech brought both excitement for what the future could hold, and trepidation for the financial burden it would place on me and my family. In my first year, I was able to get loans, grants, and scholarships, but it still wasn't enough. My whole family sacrificed and cut back on expenses. My mom worked two jobs so that I could afford the full cost.

Somewhere between when I learned English and when I applied to Virginia Tech, I decided I wanted to be an architect.

At first, I didn't realize the impact architecture had on me my entire life. Late in high school, it dawned on me how much buildings, large public spaces, and tiny nooks in the back of the library affected my day and outlook on life.

I didn't understand the joy of design until I was in architecture school. In high school, I thought I would be making houses and building for people as an architect. At Virginia Tech, I learned that thousands of tiny problems needed a solution before bringing a building to fruition. The process of solving each problem before it arises (and sometimes unfortunately after) is the heart of why I love architecture.

My first assignment at Virginia Tech was to analyze a shell and a nut. I was given a roll of paper and had to explain "what do these dissimilar items have in common?" and "what does this project have to do with architecture?"

During the first two years of school, I discovered that architecture was more than drafting a floor plan. It was looking at a problem and finding solutions—that the voids created by buildings could be made into dynamic spaces.

In school, I learned that architecture is not just a combination of art and science, but so much more. The architecture reflects our culture and creates physical environments that in turn influence our community, which in turn enhances our culture. Architecture can make everyday experiences better. Architecture, if done right, can create spaces that bring the community together, a lesson I learned as a child in El Salvador in the plaza of my basilica. A building, if designed well, can influence the well-being of the people inside.

Our profession is hard but it is rewarding. Taking time for design and the big picture while juggling a million tiny details for each project is difficult. I wake up every day enjoying what I do, and I know that none of it would be possible without all the support of my family. I took my mom's advice, and I am doing what I love. Good, thoughtful design can improve communities. I take each project, whether big or small, and look at how it can improve the community that it is part of. My biggest joy for me is to take my mom to all the places I helped design and build. It's when I walk with her in the buildings that I get my greatest joy.

My hope for the future is that I am not the only Latina in the office, the only Latina on the construction site, and the only Latina at the customer pitch meeting. In my twenty-year career, I have seen a slow change where women and minorities are coming to the profession and staying. The accumulation of disparate voices with disparate backgrounds will make both our profession and the impact of our built environment stronger. I see hope for the future. Our stories are all different and we all come to this profession adding more ways to solve problems.

UNA COSITA MÁS

Entrants into this profession can start as a drafter and grow and become an owner or a partner one day. To all of you thinking of becoming an architect, know that you are not alone; there is support from people who have lived the same struggle always ready to help. We all had to overcome people making fun of our name, and our accent, and not taking us seriously but how we deal with all our diversity is what makes us stronger. The people in this book are part of your team.

In your journey, *Haz algo que te haga feliz,* Work hard, accept all the help offered by family, friends, and your community, and keep moving forward.

And if you don't know what you want to do with your life, don't panic. This isn't a movie; sometimes you don't know when inspiration strikes until much later. Be patient; you'll figure it out.

BIOGRAPHY

Veronica Pochet received her bachelor's degree in architecture from Virginia Polytechnic Institute in 1998. As a registered architect, she has managed a wide range of projects that included academic, industrial, commercial, civic, federal, and corporate projects. She is licensed in New York, Florida, and Ohio, and has lived and worked in all three states.

She is an associate at Levin Porter Architects, A community focus design firm founded in Dayton, Ohio in 1960

Her career has included a major focus on sustainability. She is an advocate for sustainable architecture. She believes that good responsible design creates healthy spaces. Healthy spaces improve the experience of the people using the building and improves the local community.

She is proud to be among the 1% of licensed Latina architects in the U.S and is actively involved in her community. She is on the board of HATCH Architects Design Center, a K-12 nonprofit to increase diversity and architecture in the Dayton area. When she is not designing, she enjoys time with her two children and husband.

Veronica Pochet, AIA, WELL AP, LEED BD+C, CDT
Levin Porter Architects
vpochet@levin-porter.com
937.224.1931

Discovery sketches — first study abroad.

CRISTINA GALLO MCCAUSLAND

When I was seven or eight, I had a secret little notebook I carried around everywhere I went. My mom got it for me at the MoMa gift shop upon returning from one of her fantastical trips to New York City. I used it to draw the games and toys I was inventing—I imagined being a famous toy designer when I grew up.

I should've known then that I wanted to be an entrepreneur—and an architect, too, for that matter. Once I grew out of my "kids toy designer" phase and turned ten, I started collecting and crushing flowers and grasses to make my own perfume blends. I was never as entrepreneurial as my younger sister, who had a profitable business selling her cookies to the *vecinos* at age seven, but I was always making something up!

I often ask myself, how did I end up here, seven years into owning my business Via Chicago together with my husband Marty, as a licensed architect in Panama and the U.S., a world traveler for business and fun, and a mom-to-be, wondering what I dream up for myself next? When did I decide the often prescribed life of the "Latina woman," would not be mine?

I was a fifth year at the Notre Dame School of Architecture when Elizabeth McNicholas, co-founder of McNicholas Architects (back then MGLM), came to my professional practice class to speak on her experience as a business owner. Usually, the most sleep-inducing class of the week, that day I was wide-awake and furiously jotting down every word she said. Her words sparked a fire in me and that same day I set my goal to follow in her footsteps. Nowadays, Marty and I return as guest speakers for that same class every Spring—hoping to inspire others in the same way I was inspired by Elizabeth.

After graduating from the University of Notre Dame School of Architecture and being one of the few in my class to leave school with a secured job, I moved to Chicago, found an apartment, found a roommate, started my job, applied for my work permit, had a great first year at such job, made a lasting impression, and then forcefully quit my job and moved back to Panama. This all happened in twelve months.

After you graduate from an American university, you can work in the country for twelve months, opening up an opportunity to secure a job where your employer will sponsor you and apply for your H1-B 5-year work permit. It takes skill to navigate the tricky timeline, pitch yourself as an asset and not a risk while being interviewed and terrified to bring up your immigration status, and find the right employer to sponsor you, which can be expensive and time-consuming. Making sure your employer is not taking advantage of your situation and paying you a fair wage while not discounting the cost to sponsor you is a separate story and something I regret not fighting for at the time.

The H1-B process is quite gruesome. Your name is placed in a lottery system along with hundreds of thousands of other applicants, and only 65,000 names are selected randomly and awarded the five-year work visa. To state the obvious, I received a letter in the mail breaking the news that I wasn't one of the lucky 65,000 and a date by which I had to be out of the country.

The stress of navigating the immigration process can be all-consuming. After my employer applied for my work permit, I waited for the official USCIS letter to come in the mail every single day for three months. I furiously refreshed every website out there that might have some news on the statistics of this year's lottery, seeing people who were selected posting the good news (those who get selected find out first). Then the blog posts went dead silent.

Letting my employer know that I had not been selected and quitting my job was heartbreaking. Then having the news spread around the office and parting ways with the friends I made along the way was just as tough. I felt my entire future had been robbed at that moment, and there was not much else to look forward to.

Little did I know that moving to Panama was one of the

best things that ever happened to me. The day that I got the rejection letter (which by then I knew was coming thanks to my blog community of frazzled but informative applicants), I applied for a position at the same firm that I had done an internship with and received a response and offer letter within a week. I moved back in with my parents and lived at home for the next three years while getting smart about planning my future.

I transferred my college credits and got my Panama Architecture License during this time. I had long chats with my parents about starting my business someday, I gained a great network of contacts and future clients, and Marty and I dated long distance. We started a couple of side ventures like "Embassy Brewing" (home brewing with a sweet logo and extensive meeting minutes), and B.Y.O. Architecture (the Build Your Own precursor to our studio today). We signed one of our first big jobs while "moonlighting" or *"camaroneando"* as we say in Panama, and sketched logos while brainstorming ideas of what Via Chicago would become one day.

Marty and I started our company when I was twenty-five, and he was twenty-six, already married, yet I was still living in Panama waiting for my green card to arrive while he had a full-time job in Chicago. I had just given notice that I was leaving my current position as I prepared to move back to sweet home Chicago and join the Masters of Science in Real Estate (MSRE) program at Roosevelt University.

Today, I'm proud to say we've run a successful and growing business for the last seven years. Starting a business from the ground up is the most testing experience I've ever gone through and continue to navigate. Every day there are new challenges and battles to overcome. At the same time, it is also extremely rewarding and energizing—knowing that we have full autonomy and opportunity to make decisions that directly influence our daily lives.

Let's take a pause and rewind the clock to understand the motivation behind my entrepreneurial spirit: I was born in Cali, Colombia, in 1989. I'm not sharing the year of my birth to age myself. I'm sharing it because if you were raised in Cali in the early 90s, you might know how tough the city was back then. Nevertheless, I was raised in what I remember to be a very happy and loving environment.

In Colombia, our culture teaches us to work hard, figure it out as we go, and enjoy life's little moments with pleasure and dancing. Our culture is as entrepreneurial as it gets, with so many of us learning to make magic out of scratch, start something out of nothing, fail often, pick up our spirits, and start all over again.

My mom and dad started a company called RicoPastel as cake wholesalers when I was just a baby. They spent years cooking, packaging, and distributing the kind of cakes that get sold in large quantities at grocery stores, which then turn into the centerpieces of birthday celebrations. My grandmother had a thriving bakery business called Pudines Violy, named after herself, and everybody in Barranquilla knew her and her delicious sweets. My grandfather was an architect and student of LeCorbusier, whose not-so-thriving studio struggled from time to time but he always kept his passion and his pride.

When I was in high school, my mom started giving cooking classes out of our apartment, and wow, was I proud of her. I felt like she was the most famous chef of all Cali, and everybody must know my mom Chef Pachi and her world-renowned delicious cooking. I later understood she was doing this to help pay the bills and not necessarily out of passion—but she eventually found her passion as a cookbook author a few years later.

This is all to say—I come from a family that makes things happen for themselves. Since I was a teenager, my dad constantly told me, *If you want to be happy in life, don't be an employee, be independent.* My father can be haphazardly described as an unfettered workaholic, but he has taught me how to envision the most out-of-reach dreams and plan ways to make them happen.

I've been slowly learning that being Latina comes with a special set of superpowers. I've always felt like a bit of a misfit and a nomad, a self-made chameleon that is from everywhere and nowhere at the same time. Being a creative chameleon and feeling imposter syndrome can often be interchangeable. I have my bilingual, multicultural, magical realism-inspired childhood and all the wonderful places I've had the pleasure of living, studying, and dancing in to thank for that. But when I dig deep and think of who inspired me to be bold, brave, and free-spirited, I have my deep Colombian roots to thank.

Life has an infinite inventory of lessons to be learned. Hard things will happen to us, but when we pick ourselves back up, we can break through these ever-cycling tough moments and grow more resilient from our experiences.

BIOGRAPHY

Cristina Gallo, AIA, is an architect, co-founder, and President of Via Chicago, overseeing the careful execution of all design projects. She constantly forged new connections with the local community, industry partners, and future collaborators.

As a Colombian and Panamanian immigrant, Cristina drives the firm's focus on projects in Latin America and within the Spanish-speaking communities of Chicago. She acts as a translator—often literally—between the client, architect, contractor, and DOB officials and brings a lifetime of cross-cultural experience to the design process.

Cristina is currently the Vice President of "Arquitectos," a nonprofit organization with a mission to provide development, mentorship, and community assistance and further enrich the architectural profession through different cultural views and practices. She is also a mentor for "Arquitinas," a leadership and licensure initiative for Latina/x women in architecture, working to reach above and beyond the current 1% mark of licensed Latina architects in the U.S. while creating equitable and inclusive opportunities in the profession.

A University of Notre Dame graduate, Cristina also holds a Master of Science in Real Estate (MSRE) from Roosevelt University. She is a licensed architect in Illinois and the Republic of Panamá, and never, ever runs out of words.

Cristina Maria Gallo McCausland, AIA
cristina@viachicagoarchitects.com
Instagram @viachicagoarchitects

Portales was Cristina's first project in Panama, designed in 2017 and completed in 2020. This project represents the birth of Cristina's architecture studio, Via Chicago.

AN IMPORTANT DETOUR

FABIOLA YEP

I would like to begin my story on the day my life took a complete 180: the day I left Peru and began my life in the United States. This day started the most impactful chapter of my life and made me who I am today.

I remember being in the airport with my mom and my sister. I was seventeen, and all my family and closest friends came to the airport to see us off. We were coming to the states with a tourist visa and planning to stay past our allowed time. We had no idea when we would see any of them again, and I had no choice in the matter. Since I was fourteen, I knew this was the plan, but the departure date was always a moving target. I remember packing my bags for this trip. We were moving to the United States, and yet our bags needed to send the message to the U.S. Immigration Office that we were coming to visit for two weeks. I have memories of us selecting a couple of our most precious mementos and hiding them within our clothes and shoes. I remember my mom getting very upset at me because I was crying in the airport while saying my goodbyes. I understand why she was mad; after all, why would someone cry about vacationing in the United States for two weeks? Still, I couldn't help it.

Our first stop was in Houston, Texas. By that time, we had passed immigration, and we were successful at convincing our officers that we were there as tourists. At this point, the excitement of being in a new country and starting this new life had taken over. During our layover, my mom had given my sister and me $20 each to buy something at the airport, which was a lot of money for us. If given to me in Lima, I would have walked around the market for hours to ensure I got the best value. I probably would have been able to haggle a couple of clothing items, an accessory, and a good snack after my long shopping spree. However, now that I was starting this new life in the US, I told myself $20 would come around a lot easier, so I saw a key chain of a pink-colored pig with black spots and green shoes and decided that pig was worth my $20. That purchase was a direct reflection of how easy I thought my life in the United States would be. Purchases would not need to be thought about, money would not need to be stretched, and haggling would be unnecessary. During that flight, I pictured a life full of success, pride, and achievements awaiting me. What I could not detect at that moment was the very humbling and formative path I had to take to ultimately get there.

The first four years of my life in the United States were very challenging. It was not at all as breezy as I had pictured on that flight to the US. The first challenge was to get a job, so I got a job as a busser in a local TexMex restaurant, where I earned $5.15/ hr. Often, I would get into my car after double shifts and would stare at the pink-colored pig key chain with a lot of resentment. After all, earning $20 was not as easy as I had thought. Throughout those four years, I had many different jobs. I worked in restaurants, hotels, canvassing door-to-door, and cleaning agencies. Though I disliked most of those jobs, my least favorite job was working at the factory where my parents worked. The unreasonable demand in production, the unconditioned spaces, and the abusive management were hard to endure, but seeing my parents endure it daily was the hardest.

In Lima, my parents had a middle-class life. My mom, Rosa, was a stay-at-home mom. My dad, Humberto, was a store manager at a large grocery store chain, so it may be hard to understand why they decided to come to the United States; believe me that at the beginning it was hard for me to see it too, but now, eighteen years later, I know it was the right choice. Somehow, they knew they would set up a bright future for my siblings and me through that sacrifice. It also brought our family closer, and we went from enduring each other through life to becoming a team. For that sacrifice, I will be forever grateful.

When I came to the states, I had basic English knowledge but not enough to speak fluently, let alone communicate important nuances. Things like humor and wit are important for conveying your personality to others, but I did not have a command of the language to do so. However, that was not the biggest issue with my language skills. The most difficult aspect of not knowing English was having to endure people thinking I was not intelligent because I didn't yet master the English language. This often led to them patronizing me and treating me like a child. I had known I wanted to attend architecture school even before I came to the states, so naturally, when someone asked me about myself, I would define that as a future goal. However, when I mentioned it to people I had met here, I would usually get a look that would clearly state what they were thinking, like "how on earth does she think she can go to architecture school if she can't even speak English?"

My limited vocabulary was not the only reason for that reaction though. I believe people also had a hard time seeing any potential in me because of my socioeconomic background at the time. During those years, it became apparent to me that kids that grow up in a low-income or working class household were not exposed or encouraged to pursuing a professional path. As an outsider, it was very ironic to learn about the United States of America, a place where you can have the opportunity to do or become anything your heart desires, and see that this same place can also be so dismissive to a demographic of their own. I only had to live under that prejudice for four years and I was already questioning myself. I can imagine that growing up with that prejudice stops many of the most talented kids from understanding their potential. I met some of the most intelligent and kind-hearted people during those years, and though they all live lovely lives, I can't help but wonder whether they would have followed the same path if they would have been exposed to other expectations and possible goals. Nonetheless, four years went by before I was able to receive my green card and finally gain control over my future and education for the first time since moving to the U.S.

The time had come! I was starting architecture school. I was so excited that the wait was over that I didn't even realize what I was getting into when I started the program. I remember feeling very intimidated by all the other students. Many had had architecture internships or drafting and design classes in high school. A few of them even had parents that were architects who had their own firms. It was the first day and they were all proudly displaying the impressive art projects they had completed in high school. I started to question myself as much as my old coworkers. How on earth did I think I could do this? My education in Lima didn't encourage creative expression. In fact, the only artistic experiences I had were doodling on notebooks and making clothes on my sewing machine with the help of my aunt, tia Mery, my mentor and partner for any creative endeavor I wanted to take on growing up. Regardless, as intimidating as I felt coming into the architecture program, I had wanted this for too long to let that thought stop me without even trying. I remember receiving ambiguous instructions for our first project and working on it at home since I wasn't even sure I understood studio culture at the time. I came with my project covered with a trash bag. I started looking around and quickly realized that my project looked obviously different than most. I immediately thought I didn't understand the assignment. At that moment, it would be very obvious to everybody I was in way over my head and had no idea what I was supposed to be doing. They were all going to realize that I did not belong there. To my surprise, my studio teacher really liked my project. That was the first moment that I felt I was right where I was supposed to be. Throughout my years in the architecture program at Ball State University, many professors and peers challenged and encouraged me to do my best work. I went on to achieve a few awards during my time there. My studio partner and I won two out of three school competitions, and in my senior year, I was awarded a Best and Brightest scholarship for M. Arch school which is given to a few of the top undergraduate students.

Following grad school, I worked on beautiful luxury single-family homes and exclusive residential high rises, and though the end product was great, I always felt disconnected. I remember feeling so excited when I got my first job when moving to Chicago. The office was in the nicest part of Michigan avenue and just walking inside made me feel successful. A few months in, I was working late and was the only one left in the office. It was late enough that the cleaning crew came in. The cleaning crew was this one lady who spoke no English, only Spanish. I immediately recalled how my mom once had an office cleaning job and that I had to accompany her at her job because she didn't speak English. This flashback made me feel sad about where I was, not proud. It made me feel that I had too quickly turned the page on some of the most formative years of my life to now be designing spaces that people like my mother or this cleaning lady would not get to enjoy. Realizations like this made me become increasingly interested in working on projects for clients with a mission. I feel very lucky to have the opportunity to work on projects that serve people. At Wheeler Kearns Architects, I work on many educational projects where I get to design schools that I wish I would have gone to, where they encourage creativity and design. I get to design food pantries, a service my family and I used a lot in the first year of our arrival in the U.S. Most importantly, I get to use humility, empathy, and acceptance which I learned from my first 4 years in the United States in my professional life.

UNA COSITA MÁS

I believe it is up to us to find value in all the experiences we have. When we are put into situations that we have no control over, it's important to focus on what you do have control over, such as, what can you learn from it? How can you help it or prevent it from happening in the future? This way you will have gained something once the storm has passed. I feel extremely grateful for the struggles I have experienced and I feel very proud of the outlook I have gained from them. I'm now personally and professionally committed to help expose people to their full potential. This reflects itself in my passion for mentoring or my strive to design dignified spaces that inspire underserved communities.

BIOGRAPHY

Originally from Lima, Peru, Fabiola Yep is a licensed architect that aims to enrich communities through her designs, mentoring, volunteering, and equity efforts. Her empathetic approach to design focuses on learning the core values and core needs of the client from the get-go to be prepared to guide and support them throughout the entire architectural process. She currently works at Wheeler Kearns Architects (WKA), a Chicago-based architecture firm. At WKA, she has led various educational and community-focused projects that serve communities in need. As an immigrant, she recognizes the importance of guidance and representation, which are the main drivers of her passion for mentorship. She is an active mentor in many different organizations, such as Big Brother Big Sisters, Ace Mentorship and Arquintina.

Fabiola Yep, AIA
Fabiola@wkarch.com
https://www.linkedin.com/in/fabiola-yep-aia-449818107/

HAY HERMANAS, MUCHÍSIMO QUE HACER

PATRICIA G. ALARCÓN

It will only be for a year; let's give it a try.

That's how my parents sold our family's move from Lima, Perú to Birmingham, Alabama when I was just eleven years old. To be fair, I was born in Baltimore, Maryland, where my parents were completing their studies, but we moved back to Lima when I was just four years old. I'd promptly forgotten any English I might have spoken and any memory of my early childhood years.

As far as I could remember, Lima was the only home I'd ever known, and I was not at all convinced about leaving it. But a short-term stint in the U.S. could be an adventure, an opportunity not to be passed up. After all, in Perú and among our family and friends, the U.S. was seen as a mecca, the land of opportunity where anything was possible. Without much more discussion (because really, did the kids have a say in this decision?), we packed up our bags and moved from Lima to Birmingham on Jan. 8, 1980.

[Side note: Other immigrants may relate to this; the date when you leave your homeland to make your way to a new place stays with you forever, and it becomes a marker in your life, a divide between your life before and your life after. For a long time, I rationalized that I could still consider myself more Peruvian than American as long as I'd spent more of my life in Perú than in the U.S. When the balance shifted, the question of identity became more poignant. Was I American or Peruvian? Both or neither? It is the immigrant's dilemma.]

A lifetime later, because that year in the U.S. became two, then three, then four until we stopped asking about when we were going back, and I have embraced my life as a bi-cultural Peruvian-American, proudly and firmly straddling two cultures.

From the beginning, we maintained strong ties to Perú, where we have a large extended family. Coming from Lima, the capital city and a bustling urban metropolis, to Birmingham, by comparison, a small city that is more suburb than downtown, was an extreme culture shock. At first, the daily struggle was relearning the language and trying to fit in.

While I was initially unaware of Birmingham's infamous place in the history of the Civil Rights movement, I did experience a city that was still segregated. And in a world of black and white, it was hard to figure out where this Latina kid transplanted to the Deep South could fit in. We were different, and in our suburban development, we were "the Peruvian family" among our primarily white neighbors, who gratefully and, for the most part, made us feel welcome. However, there was always the sense of being on the outside.

The beauty of "let's try this for a year" is that whatever you're going through, especially the difficult times, becomes more bearable, knowing that it's only temporary and that, eventually, you will return to more familiar and safe territory. It's a security blanket. I can make it through this or that because I am not staying here; this is not my home. I am going back. But after some time, I settled into my new life in the U.S. I found my people in high school and started focusing on college and the road ahead, as is the ritual for many American teenagers (those privileged enough to have college in their sights).

I'M GOING TO BE AN ARCHITECT.

My parents came to the U.S. to further their careers and, just as importantly, to expand educational and job opportunities for my siblings and me. When choosing my career path, architecture was a very rational decision and also a bit of a rebel move. You see, my parents are both physicians, and it was somewhat expected, maybe as much by them as by me, that as their firstborn, I would follow in their footsteps. But I get weak-kneed at the sight of blood and almost threw up dissecting our fetal pig in high school biology. So, no, a career in medicine was not in the cards.

Lucky for me, I had a "cousin" in Birmingham [in quotes because he's not my cousin by blood, but my Peruvian community in Birmingham was so small that everyone was a tía, tío, or primo, blood lineage be damned]. Anyway, my primo who had switched from pre-med and was studying architecture opened my eyes to a career outside the medical profession. He'd come home for holidays and showed me what he was working on—fantastical drawings, sculptural wooden models, and imaginary worlds. I was intrigued. To this day, whenever I visit Birmingham, I stop by his studio to see what he's working on; he is always animated and excited about his craft. He would become one of my earliest mentors.

But let's go back to the moment I decided I would not pursue a career in medicine. I have already talked about my uneasiness with the labs in my high school biology class. What I really loved were my art classes as well as my physics and math coursework. I started to think that architecture could be a field where I could do both: be creative and expressive and analytical and rational.

It was the summer of my junior year in high school; I was working as a research assistant in a lab, still thinking maybe there was a track for me in medicine, when I ran into one of my mother's colleagues who asked point blank if I was going to be a doctor, "just like your parents." I thought about it for a minute, thought queasily of the blood samples that I had placed in the autoclave earlier in the day, and declared that no, in fact, I was not going to be a doctor, and said, "I am going to be an architect," end of story. He seemed satisfied with my response and shuffled off. But more importantly, I was satisfied with my response. It's as if I'd tried it on for size, and it fit just right.

I liked the idea of becoming an architect and ran with it. I recognize that I have been lucky and privileged. Lucky, because my parents supported my dreams unconditionally and privileged because college was not just an option but the natural expectation of how my life in America would unfold.

To be fair, I had no idea what I was getting into or what it really meant to be an architect in any practical terms, but I stuck with it. When it came time to apply to colleges, I only considered those with strong undergraduate architectural programs; and I ended up going to Washington University in St. Louis.

Going away to college is a quintessentially American experience. In Lima at the time, if you were fortunate enough to attend university, you did so in Lima. You lived at home, never experiencing the independence many American teens are forced to exercise when they leave home. This was the only tradition I'd known, and leaving home at eighteen was another major shift in my life; a long way for the Limeña from Birmingham to go, yet again.

CORAJE, CARAJO.

Architecture school kicked my a**, and I loved it. I loved the camaraderie with my classmates, resulting from endless hours in studio. While initially intimidated by the blank page at the beginning of each project, once I landed on an idea, I was all-in to iterate and explore it. That is not to say that there weren't many moments of self-doubt, anxiety, and questioning whether I had what it took to make it through the program or whether

I belonged there in the first place. Doubts, which anyone in a creative field can likely relate to, can be quite paralyzing. You're staring at your canvas, trace, or model, and you just can't envision your next move. In those moments of darkness, I would confide in friends, parents, and counselors. I was (and am) fortunate to have such a support network. On one such occasion, I was despairing about how a project was or rather was not going, and I was lamenting about it on the phone with my mom.

I haven't told you much about her yet, but my mom is formidable. I've never had to look too far for an example of someone who inspires me because she's been my constant, my north star, guiding me in my path. She's a leader in her field of rheumatology, specializing in lupus research, a great teacher to generations of physicians here in the U.S. and all over Latin America, and loyal to the core.

At eighty years old, she continues to be passionate about her work and dedicated to mentoring. She's incredibly generous and pragmatic and doesn't take any B.S. I am in awe of her work ethic and commitment (even in retirement!), not because of a desire for recognition or financial reward but because of her enduring *amor al arte,* love of the craft. She's the rock of our family, solid and steady, and I am blessed every day that I have her in my life.

On that particular day, in the thick of the semester with a crit looming, I had been fretting about my work when she stopped me with two simple words: *Coraje, carajo!* Courage, damn it! This was way before FaceTime, but I could still feel the power of her words reaching me through the phone line, snapping me out of my bout of self-pity. She wasn't mean or angry, but with those words, she reminded me that I had the strength to get through it, that I needed to dig deep, and that it was ultimately up to me to find my way out.

Eventually, I printed those words and pinned them above my studio desk. I referred to them often in those moments of doubt, a reminder that I could do it and that I had it in me. I eventually graduated from WashU with honors and continued my graduate studies at UC Berkeley. In retrospect, I can see that my mom was building me up, not with empty praise but with an empowering message of self-reliance, resilience, and perseverance. Not only *si se puede,* it can be done, but *si tu puedes.* YOU can do it.

GRAB A SEAT.

By now, I have been practicing architecture for over twenty-five years, and in that time, I have been fortunate to work on some wonderful projects with amazing teams and clients. And no matter how you slice it, this is still primarily a white, male-dominated field. And though we continue to make strides, the challenge of representation for women and people of color across the profession, especially in leadership, is as important today as it was when I graduated.

For years, it was easier to put my head down and focus on the work, reminding myself that that's what's important. Our work can be impactful and make a difference. And that was enough. But it was also discouraging when I did look up not seeing anyone like me reflected in leadership positions and no clear path for how that could change.

But sometimes, you only need a small opportunity to change the narrative. One day, one of our associate principals mentioned a weekly marketing meeting, and if anyone was interested, feel free to come by. I am not sure how genuine that invitation was, but when the time came, I grabbed my notebook and made my way to the meeting room. The regular attendees, already seated, looked at me, puzzled. I reminded them of the open invitation to attend, which was followed by an awkward silence. Then without skipping a beat, the marketing director who would later become my dear friend and trusted confidant, moved over, made room for me, and said, "Sure, grab a seat!" And with that, resumed the conversation.

I continued to make my way to the weekly meeting, quiet at first, then gaining more confidence and eventually becoming an active participant, strategizing on pursuits, teaming opportunities, and client outreach. That simple gesture of literally making room at the table led to my sense of belonging, to a growing involvement in the practice, and to the leadership role I hold today. I am grateful to those who have made room for me and am reminded to do so for others, to lift as we climb.

I can see now that the decision to "just try it for a year" had a profound impact on the trajectory of my life. What would life be like if we had never left Perú? Where would I be today? Would I have found my way to architecture? Because of my life as a Peruvian-American growing up in the Deep South, I have experienced a sense of "otherness," of not belonging, or of being just on the outside. That in turn has led me to this simple truth:

representation matters, and having diverse voices *"in the room where it happens"* makes for richer outcomes.

I am keenly aware that oftentimes some voices are left out of the conversation when it comes to design. I am committed to increasing representation, broadening the conversation, and working with our clients to develop inclusive and welcoming places that promote a sense of belonging. I love that because of the public nature of my work, I get to work with many to positively impact the lives of others. And I realize that this moment, this place, and this profession is exactly where I am supposed to be. *Adelante!* Onward.

UNA COSITA MÁS

I grew up in typical Latin American fashion with many *refránes,* one proverb for every occasion. But one which sticks with me is a saying my father had framed above his desk in his study (and it was always there, no matter where we lived). It is by the Peruvian poet, César Vallejo, and it said simply, *"Hay hermanos, muchísimo que hacer."* or translated, "There is, my brothers, so much [left] to do." It is such a simple sentence, universally understood and loaded with a resolute sense of urgency, that pushes you forward no matter your path, with the knowledge that our time is limited, and we mustn't waste it. I also interpret it to mean that humans are imperfect works-in-progress, always learning and evolving. There is an inherent optimism that we can and must do better.

I'd like to think that I have taken this saying to heart and carry it with me, much like my father has for a lifetime. Often it makes me impatient for change. But I have also learned that change doesn't just happen; you can't only wish it to happen. You have to make it happen. To that end, I urge you never to be afraid to be the squeaky wheel and to advocate for yourself and others. It may not always be easy; it may even be scary, but there is power in speaking out and standing up for what you believe in.

Lastly, don't be afraid to seize the opportunity when it presents itself. All you need is a crack to hold the proverbial door open and walk right in. And once you do, keep it open and help others walk on through. As Vice President Kamala Harris said so eloquently in her acceptance speech, when we are the first, we also need to make sure we're not the last. *Hay hermanas, muchísimo que hacer.* There is, my sisters, so much left to do.

BIOGRAPHY

A Ratcliff's Academic Practice leader, Patricia focuses on creating student-centered environments that elevate and transform the learning experience and build community.

With a career spanning twenty five-plus years, she has worked on new facilities and renovations on K-12 and higher education campuses. With an eye towards successful outcomes, she is committed to engaging broadly and listening deeply, recognizing the value of diversity of thought and experience and the institutional knowledge and insight her clients bring to each project. She is committed to designing for inclusion and fostering a sense of welcoming and belonging in the environments she helps to realize.

Patricia understands the big picture and is mindful of the day-to-day efforts required to meet project goals, budgets, and schedules. Skilled at managing projects of varying scales and complexity, she works closely with multiple stakeholders in all design phases, from early visioning to programming and planning, managing expectations and decision-making to keep projects on track.

A firm leader committed to fostering a more equitable and just practice, Patricia founded Ratcliff's Equity, Diversity, and Inclusion (REDI) group, whose efforts include expanding the firm's commitment to its local community, reviewing firm practices through an equity lens, and implementing changes that continue to move the EDI-needle forward within Ratcliff and beyond.

Patricia G. Alarcón, AIA

palarcon@ratcliffarch.com

510-899-6400

Concept sketches for new building in Jenner, California. Studies in creating a welcoming sense of place through siting, scale, massing, and materiality.

HOMER A. PEREZ,

Believing in yourself, living the mantra of "Anything is Possible," and keeping engaged with your community have been principles of my life I have practiced that have helped throughout my career.

I grew up on the Inner West Side of San Antonio, TX. I guess you would call it the Barrio. That neighborhood had the worst school district in the country at that time. An only child, I still had the amazing warmth and love of a close-knit traditional Mexican-American Family. My grandmothers were 3 blocks from each other. Most of my relatives lived very close to one another, so there was a lot of family community and gatherings. Growing up in that environment didn't make me feel impoverished or "less than others." It gave me the confidence that I could do whatever I wanted.

When I got to elementary school, I was deep into my academics because it was my escape from the neighborhood, and

I learned new ways of thinking. I got exposed to different things like music, art, and mathematics, which was magical for a fifth grader. My mom was a topographic map draftsperson at the time for a local survey company, and I would sketch under her desk when she had to work late. Her manager noticed my sketches, and he said I had a good hand. Those were the beginnings of my career in architecture and design.

Understanding I was excelling in my studies, my parents sacrificed and put me in private school for the rest of my schooling—and I did not take it for granted. Again, academics became my escape from the neighborhood, and as a teenager, there were many opportunities for trouble. In high school, I took my first architectural rendering class at my mom's suggestion and met my first architect.

It was a pencil rendering class, and I was impressed by the subject matter and inspired by the instructor, so I would stay a little later to learn more about his profession. With the attitude of "Anything is Possible," I was accepted into the Massachusetts Institute of Technology, even though my Anglo-American Academic Advisor said I wouldn't be accepted. I was the first person in my blood family to go to college, and it was MIT. Again, anything is possible if you believe in yourself.

At MIT, I, ironically, was studying computer science. Computers were new in the late 80s/early 90s, and I was fascinated with them. I decided to pursue computer science; however, the major was also accompanied by electrical engineering. With the encouragement of my peers, I took some courses in architecture because they saw my sketching and space-planning skills.

One year I got accepted to an internship at IBM in East Fishkill, NY, and spent the summer enjoying upstate New York and producing code for large mainframe computers. At the end of the internship, my supervisor told me I was way too creative for computer science and would be depressed if I stayed on that career path. I went back to MIT and switched my major to architecture. MIT has the oldest architecture school in the country. It was then that my career started to bud.

In my new major, I excelled, and I found my niche. What I love about architecture is that it combines art and science. You are also helping your community by providing shelter and protecting them from the elements and doing it beautifully by designing structures that make your community feel good while being protected.

I managed to complete the three-year program in two years. I lived off of four twenty-minute naps per day my senior year, but I did it because I did not want to accumulate another year's tuition debt, and my parents were helping support me, and I could not have them sacrifice any longer.

With the mantra of keeping engaged with my community, I was accepted into a position for a Ph.D. student project, which was preparing for the 1993 AIA National Convention in Boston. He would prove that computers can be used in architecture (what a concept!). Because of my computer science background, I became part of the team, even though I was an undergraduate.

This was the beginning of computer-aided design. We created three-dimensional shapes in CAD and created an algorithm so the computer could generate bridge structures with the shapes we input into the computer. We then rendered the bridge structures, adding scale figures and perspective views. The views were printed onto a long blueprint exhibited at the convention.

The rest is history, and now I can't imagine what we would do without computer technology in architecture and design. When I graduated with a BS in architecture, I graduated in a recession. I had my degree and spoke four languages, but I could not find a job on the East Coast or in Europe. So I moved back to San Antonio, where my unforeseen retail architecture career began.

One of my main inspirations in architecture is Santiago Calatrava. I am one of his biggest fans, even though his projects are always over budget! I adore him because he is what I have always wanted to be: an architect, structural engineer, and sculptor. The man is amazing in my eyes.

I took engineering courses and ceramics at a local community college when I returned to San Antonio. Again, keeping the mantra of "believe in yourself," I took a job at a small structural engineering firm as a CAD monkey. Still, it allowed me to be mentored by my structural engineer peers and understand the basic concepts of structural engineering. Then, one day on a job site where my boss (Bill) and my future boss (Bill) were fighting to complete a structural detail where a wood-framed glulam beam roof would meet a new steel-framed expansion roof. I approached them and suggested a solution, and my future boss looked at me and said, "Who are you?" The next thing I knew, I got a call from the future Bill and accepted a position with this Store Design team.

The food retail company was HEB Grocery Company, and they were founded in 1905, have fierce brand loyalty, and their territory at the time was mostly in Texas. I was hired as a store designer and managed specific site projects, store prototype designs, and design guidelines for specific store departments. I didn't realize how complicated grocery store retail design can be. There are a lot of MEP items to coordinate, and you also have to deal with the customer experience on top of designing the storefront, which sometimes can be very wide, so you have to really think about how you articulate those storefronts because you are limited to fenestration (i.e., where you can place windows).

After a couple of years of working on domestic projects, Bill asked me if I would work in Mexico to open stores designed for the Mexican consumer along the Northern border of Mexico in Monterrey. I accepted without hesitation! Starting at the moment, I would drive to a private hangar on Monday mornings, get on the private jet with HEB Leadership, and fly to Monterrey, where we would be taken in a bulletproof wagon to the HEB Mexico Corporate Headquarters. I would work at the headquarters the week and fly back on Thursday. I felt like a rock star.

The amazing thing about working abroad is you learn how

other cultures interact and experience communities you can't find in the U.S. I highly recommend in your career that you study or intern abroad or work abroad at least once to experience what is outside of the familiar. This was part of the reason I went to MIT, and it was 2,000 miles from my hometown.

While working in Mexico, I opened fifteen of the first sixteen stores from Matamoros to Monterrey. It was my first exposure to design-build projects, and it was intense. Still, I learned a lot about providing on-site design solutions, addressing the needs of my internal cross-functional teams and the customer, and doing it in a different language. I also had to deal with some "Indiana Jones" experiences walking on job sites with exposed conduit, lighting installers dangling from roof joists, and open penetrations without protection. It was magical. My Spanish also got an upgrade, and by the time I left HEB, I spoke formal social and technical Spanish fluently. It was such a gift and still helps me today. I cannot stress the importance of being bilingual enough, especially in the architecture/construction industry. It was at that time that I decided to get my architect's license, so it was time to continue on my next chapter.

I moved to San Francisco in 2001 to continue my professional design career and FIND LOVE! I have been with my Life Partner now for twenty years and still going strong! I was going to try a different building type to judge if it was appropriate for me, but I ended up back in retail—this time, it was national retail. I joined McCall Design Group and, using my attitude of "believe in yourself," I told my Principal that I would not join his firm UNLESS he allowed me to work on construction documents and construction details. My career had mostly been in store design and I could read construction documents but had never produced a set of drawings. He started me out, of course, in design, where I helped create a new brand for Williams-Sonoma, Inc. Brand store design is different based on the type of retailer it is; remember that.

The nuances of luxury brand store design were introduced to me. After that epic exercise, I got into the weeds and created a set of prototype template construction documents for this new brand. I eventually got to project manage new stores across the country, including larger flagship formats.

I began getting a little bored with the day-to-day project management/drawing schedule, so I investigated the U.S. Green Building Council's LEED Rating System and became LEED Accredited in 2005. From then on, I became very engaged in the green building industry. Eventually, I became the head of our firm's Green Team, assisting with the LEED for Retail Pilot Program and assisting our clients on how to be kinder to the Planet. I eventually got my license in 2011 and said goodbye to McCall Design Group to begin another chapter in "divergent practice."

"Divergent practice" = using your skill set for other possible career alternatives. I joined Moss, Inc. in 2011 and assisted in creating a retail division of their company. They specialized in the temporary installation of tension fabric products that would be anything from advertisements to full environmental structures for all kinds of events and conferences. I was hired because I understood the built environment, permanent installation requirements for retail, and my retail contacts. I was one of four, and within three years, we were contributing 60 million dollars of revenue and went from four to 60 people in our division. I became Director of Design and was allowed to work from home, as did my account executives. Being in manufacturing, I could start my own practice and do small retail/mercantile projects on the side. My Director role became very demanding, so I returned to retail architecture after three years. Ironically, I got a call from Sephora, the luxury beauty retailer, and accepted a position as Senior Store Design Project Manager, where I currently hold my hat and continue my retail architecture career.

Being in the Bay Area for over twenty years has provided me with an abundance of opportunities, not just on a professional level but on a personal level. I am deeply connected with my building industry network and have helped found the Latinx in Architecture Committee of the AIA San Francisco Chapter, which brings education, scholarships, and networking to the Latinx community in the Bay Area and throughout the country.

I continue to mentor the younger Latinx generations and hopefully inspire them to enter a design profession because our Latinx communities represent a substantial part of our country's population. We should have design professionals building communities and structures that appeal to those communities with equity and sustainability in mind. I hope the younger generations reading my story will be inspired to believe in themselves, live the mantra of anything is possible, and give back / support your community.

UNA COSITA MÁS

Even though I live in San Francisco, a food-lovers dream city, you can't find good TexMex or Texas BBQ here. Believe me, I have looked wide and far! So when I go back to San Antonio to visit my family, one of the things I like most is EAT! Pan dulce from Bedoy's, breakfast tacos from Taco Haven, empanadas and fish tacos from Beto's Alt Mex, tortilla soup and enchiladas from Rosario's and Texas BBQ from Rudy's! It fills my heart with joy and brings back so many memories of my childhood.

"Feel the fear and do it anyway!"

If English is not your first language, never give up your native language. Spanish was my first language, and growing up bilingual was a huge benefit. I now speak four languages and dabble with three other languages. With the world becoming smaller and more connected, I have learned that spoken language has benefited my career and personal life. Language is connection on any level. I always encourage younger generations to keep speaking the languages they know and practice them because, eventually, that skill will come in their favor in their career or journey in life.

BIOGRAPHY

A fourth-generation Mexican-American, Homer A. Perez was born in San Antonio, TX, in 1971. He grew up on the Inner West Side, one of the city's most neglected areas. Excelling in his studies, he attended the Massachusetts Institute of Technology where he studied architecture. After graduating in a recession, he moved back to San Antonio and joined the Design Team at HEB Grocery Company, a food retailer whose region was Texas. In 1996, HEB placed him in Mexico to design stores addressing the Mexican consumer. HEB and Homer introduced ADA to Mexico.

In 2001, he moved to San Francisco and continued in retail architecture, supporting brands such as Nike, Williams-Sonoma, and Sephora. He became a LEED Accredited Professional in 2005 and collaborated on the LEED for Retail Pilot Program. In 2010, he was named "Top 20 Under 40" by the Retail Design Industry.

Homer possesses thirty years of experience in retail and sustainable design. He is a licensed architect in California and Texas and a LEED AP with a Building Design + Construction credential. Homer has been a member of AIA National since 2001. He helped found the committee Latinx in Architecture in 2013 and supports the Chicano Architecture Student Association at the University of California at Berkeley. He is currently a Senior Store Design Project Manager at Sephora, the Luxury Beauty Company, and is Sephora's LVMH Sustainable Store Planning Ambassador.

Homer A. Perez, AIA, NOMA, LEED BD+C
homerinsf@gmail.com
twitter:@homerinsf

ALZIRA MALDONADO PROTSISHIN

Architects can shape the built environment that directly impacts our communities. I have always been drawn to the idea of improving people's lives through the built environment.

I was born in Kyiv, Ukraine (formerly the Soviet Union), to a Ukrainian mom and a Colombian father. My parents met in college while both were pursuing an engineering degree. When I was three, we moved to Colombia, where I grew up, and it was my home for the next twenty-five years.

After moving, my mom started studying Spanish while taking care of me and helping at my grandparents' bookstore during the day. She had bigger dreams of finding a job as an engineer. After all, she had a bachelor's and a master's degree and was determined to put them to use. Shortly after, she found a job as a structural engineer at a consulting firm, where her journey as an engineer in another country started.

My parents split in my early childhood, and I lived with my mom. Later, both of my parents remarried, and I spent my childhood between both households. My home was always a mix of cultures and ideals, and listening to my mom's stories of 'back home' always made me question the idiosyncrasies of our society. When my mom remarried (another structural engineer), they bought a house that was split in half by a concrete wall. The previous house owners had gotten an ugly divorce where they didn't want to leave the house to the other party, so they decided to build a wall in the middle and be neighbors. Moving into this house was fascinating as now we had all these plans to transform our house to our needs!

I grew up on what felt like a permanent 'construction site' with all the improvements and remodeling we did to our home throughout the years. Planning and drawing the remodeling and later seeing the improvements to our home was like playing with estralandia (LEGO for buildings) but in real life. I would also usually go to construction sites with them and see drawings hanging on the studio walls and structural models of buildings or bridges on their screens. I saw many projects come to life, from housing to constructing a pedestrian bridge over a busy six-lane highway that people previously had to run across in their daily commute.

At a young age, I had my son, Juan. This made me start thinking about the next generation and my role in the big picture of society as an individual, a mother, and a contributing person to our future. Seeing firsthand the positive impact on the community while visiting construction sites with my parents and witnessing my own with all the improvements to our home and how it changed how we used the spaces. I knew early on that I wanted to be an architect, and I wanted to be part of this group of people dedicated to improving the quality of life of others.

Did I doubt it right before going to school because the 'destiny' of an architect in my country was to be a taxi driver? Indeed, I did! There was a common society saying that architects could not make any money and ended up as taxi drivers to provide for their families. That was scary! At the time, I loved chemistry class at school. I did really well, so I decided to apply to a chemical engineering school… but after being accepted, I doubted myself again. I was pursuing a career because I thought I could find better jobs in the future and not because it was really my passion. Next semester I decided to apply to architecture school, where my journey as an architect finally started!

My experience during the first years in architecture school was that it was hard work! I did not always have the best grades or truly understand the tasks. Design studios were time-consuming and really demanding. I doubted myself again if this was my true calling. I felt that I was behind and just not getting it. That I was approaching the tasks in the wrong way. I was trying to solve the architecture with the tools I was learning but not interpreting the big idea or gesture and using those tools later to solve it.

In my third year, I finally started to understand that there was something else in the approach to the tasks. This sensibility and joy had been developing over the last couple of years that I was starting to grasp, allowing me to dream big and later resolve. Today I reflected on this and understood what architecture school was about. It was not about the task but the creative process of solving the problem; it was not the 'amount of time' it took, it was about the outstanding creative solution. There is not a correct solution as there might be several; it is only the creative process that results in a solution reflecting our involvement in that process and our thinking behind it.

After graduating with a bachelor's degree in architecture and working for three years, in different architectural firms, I fell short of my dream of impacting communities through my work and the opportunities to grow professionally. My mom had recently been transferred to an office in the states, so I also decided to pursue my dream in the land of opportunities. I knew that a better education would give me access to those opportunities, so I decided to study English as a second language and prepare for the GRE to apply to schools in the U.S. A short year later, I was admitted to a master of architecture program at the Illinois Institute of Technology.

This was my second chance to do great in school and absorb everything I could, with the only caveat that this time the classes were in English. I had just moved to a city where I didn't know anyone, and I had to take care of my son too. I have to say that it was not easy, in a different way from undergraduate school, as this time, I knew how to approach school. Still, it took me longer to do the tasks in English, like writing essays or understanding building systems, and this time I didn't have the family support I had back home, so my hours a day always felt short.

I really enjoyed going back to school. It was so much fun to study in a different city than the one I grew up in and especially in Chicago where the city architecture is full of history and multicultural heritage. I meet people from different countries and backgrounds that open my eyes to a diversity of approaches and ideals to architecture.

While I was in school, I started looking for internships so I could have experience working in the states and later have the possibility to find a job after graduation. I knew I wanted to remain in the states to access better opportunities, so I needed a job and a work visa sponsorship.

In my second year in graduate school, I started working at EXP as an intern. I remember being busy as a full-time mom, student, and part-time intern. Life was busy, but I was working on interesting projects and gaining the desired experience. Upon graduation, I joined EXP, an architecture and engineering consulting firm with headquarters in Chicago, where I have been able to harness my skills as a designer, allowing me to work on many high-profile projects in architecture around the states. Nine years later, I still work at the same office and enjoy every project that lands in my desk.

I've had the opportunity to work on several public projects that have harvested my passion for public architecture. I have been involved in many high-profile infrastructure projects and a new United States courthouse, where my objective to contribute to communities through the built environment is fostered.

In 2021, I was awarded the AIA Chicago Dubin Family Young Architect Award. This was an exciting and, at the same time, mind-blowing event. Not only because I had been looking up to this award as a recognition for my hard work but also as a reassurance that I was doing something right. This award opened the door for me to reach out to others to tell my story and inspire the new generations. I have also gotten to know many people in the community from whom I have learned as friends and colleagues. One of the most exciting groups I got to join is Arquitina! I have never met so many Latin women in the industry that are fearless to pursue they dreams.

I have to say that I highly value the mentors around me. Throughout my career, I have connected with other professionals who mentored me and helped me navigate the profession in the U.S. They have helped me grow in the profession and my personal life. Since, it has been my drive to continue with the legacy and give back to the profession by mentoring young professionals through different organizations where I serve as a mentor. And the most rewarding part is that mentorship is a two-way street learning experience.

UNA COSITA MÁS

I couldn't have a better role model than my mom. My mom is a strong woman who has reshaped her life not once but twice outside her native country. She moved to Colombia with a toddler without knowing the language. She learned Spanish so she could work and give me the best life she could. I saw her work hard as a structural engineer in a men's world and work her way up. Little did she know she would face the same challenge again, but here in the states and she took it again. She moved here knowing little English and was studying to learn the language while working. Today she is a licensed structural engineer in three countries.

Seeing firsthand the challenges and efforts it took my mom to navigate two different cultures has shaped me into the woman I am today. I have never seen her give up on anything, and I haven't either. Her example gave me the confidence that I could do it too.

My advice: Have a plan for what you want to achieve, and always have that vision in your mind. It doesn't matter the color, the shape, the package, or how and when it will materialize. Take the efforts individually, and if your decisions are made from the heart, even if that plan doesn't appear as you envisioned it, the outcome will always be bright and true to your heart.

BIOGRAPHY

Alzira Maldonado Protsishin, AIA, the AIA Chicago 2021 Young Architect Award winner, is a Senior Design Architect at EXP, where, for the past nine years, she has focused her career on work in the public realm to make design excellence accessible to all. She has been a key contributor to some of the firm's highest profile / award-winning projects, including the Washington/Wabash Elevated Station, the 95th Street/Dan Ryan Intermodal Terminal Station, and the US Courthouse in Saipan, Commonwealth of the Northern Mariana Islands.

Alzira earned her bachelor's degree in architecture from the University of Los Andes in Bogota, Colombia, and a master's degree in architecture from the Illinois Institute of Technology in Chicago. She serves as a mentor in Arquitina, the AIA Chicago WING program, and the AIA Chicago Foundation diversity program.

Alzira Maldonado Protsishin, AIA

LinkedIn: /alzira-maldonado-protsishin/

Northern Mariana Islands United States Courthouse in Saipan. A design of a new US Courthouse that reconciles the monumental language of a significant public building with the specific local culture, site and context of the island.

PERMANENT FOREIGNER, A CITIZEN OF THE WORLD

FRANCISCO J. RODRÍGUEZ-SUÁREZ

I grew up in Puerto Rico, an island that is politically part of the U.S., geographically part of the Caribbean, culturally part of Latin America, and historically an intriguing synthesis between Europe, Africa, and native Taíno. I have always been fascinated by the creative possibilities of the hybrid condition. I ultimately chose the only discipline that lies precisely at the intersection of science and the humanities, of arts and technology—architecture.

My father emigrated from Spain; my mother is puertorriqueña; I have spent most of my life between San Juan, Madrid, and the U.S. Admittedly, I have experienced this curious journey as a permanent foreigner, but also a citizen of the world, with two colonial passports and marked accents in every language. Nobody is a prophet in his own land.

Like many architects, I spent my childhood doodling and playing with LEGO. Years later, my sons Sebastián and Gustavo reminded me that I was privileged to make a living doing just that as an adult.

I also remember going to Old San Juan as a kid and visiting El Morro fortress, where I flew kites with my younger brother Jorge and had cold piraguas to deal with the heat and humidity of those endless summers. Walking through the cobblestoned streets with colored facades and picturesque balconies provided a unique exposure to the virtues of urban life, conspicuously absent in the suburban sub-divisions that aspired to a misconstrued version of the American Dream while ironically calling themselves *urbanizaciones*.

In retrospect, that grid surrounded by a perimeter wall felt like an ideal city, and even then, I could tell it was different, the same way that my high school buildings also felt unique. I later found out that those simple Modernist edifices were designed by Henry Klumb, a German émigré who had previously worked for Frank Lloyd Wright and was hired by the Jesuits to give form to the Colegio San Ignacio. Little did I know then that I would spend much of my life surrounded by Klumb's remarkable buildings as a professor at the University of Puerto Rico.

I must confess that I was—and still am—fascinated by airplanes and flying. I would design planes, but also airports. Perhaps that explains why I originally applied to Georgia Tech, obsessed with the idea of studying aerospace engineering. My father, who always leaned towards architecture even though he is more of an engineer type, suggested I visit the School of Architecture building. Eventually, I did. Reminiscing about that day, I am convinced, as my mother would say, that the universe conspires to lead you to the right path, whatever that may be. I immediately became enamored with the beautifully complex drawings and models from a student exhibition. At that moment, I asked to switch majors, and somehow, I was allowed to enroll in architecture, where I ostensibly found my true calling.

As an undergrad at Tech, I practically lived in the design studios contiguous to Jim Williamson's two Hejduk masques and was passionate about Betty Dowling's architectural history class. I remember pulling all-nighters with my classmates, Ili Hidalgo and Luly Bestard, two talented Latina architects from Puerto Rico and Miami. Those nights the whole world ceased to exist as we engaged in an unrehearsed ritual with the ethos of the creative process. Anything was possible as the first marks of ink and graphite explored empty pieces of paper. Suddenly, the calibrated communion between form and space began to make sense.

Between my Freshman and Sophomore years, I went to Madrid with my friend José Ernesto Mieres, who had decided to leave a computer science major at Georgia Tech to study philosophy instead. After a few days, we got a summer job teaching English to Spanish students so that we could stay the entire summer. While I had visited my father's family on various occasions, I was experiencing the city on my own terms this time. Those days were certainly formative as we met interesting people who discussed, debated, and speculated about life's fundamental questions and our roles within those paradigms. For the most part, we listened to The Beatles, but that summer, we also met Silvio Rodríguez, both figuratively and literally. Nothing would ever be the same.

During our fourth year, I crossed the Atlantic once again, this time to France, where Tech offered its study abroad program. As a young man, Ernest Hemmingway knew that Paris was 'a moveable feast.' While living at the *Cité Universitaire,* we walked, drew, and visited buildings, spaces, and monuments. The atmosphere was undeniably cosmopolitan, sophisticated, and intellectual as we read Italo Calvino, Umberto Eco, and Milan Kundera, watched international cinema, and attended exhibitions and even ballet at Garnier's Opera. Occasionally, we would even understand a few sentences in French, which was certainly easier for those of us who also spoke Spanish.

On weekends, we would use—and abuse—our Eurail passes and hop on overnight trains, mostly to Spain or Italy, accompanied by tight backpacks, sketchbooks, baguettes, and, when we were lucky, cheap wine. Traveling without iPhones, email, social media (or free calls on WhatsApp) was quite different from today's hyper-documented and ever-present experiences. We spent most of the time devouring books about the cities, buildings, and architects we were about to witness. It was imperative to know precedents, and we did. My lowly bank account was hardly ever out of the red. Fortunately, we didn't need much to be happy. Pencil and paper usually sufficed, and they still do.

In 1992, it was an exciting year for architecture that provided us with plenty of interesting destinations. Mitterrand transformed Paris with his Grand Projects, including la Defense, IM Pei's Louvre pyramid and Jean Nouvel's Institute du Monde Arab. Interestingly, Paris continued to allow for innovation, ever since the Eiffel Tower to the Pompidou Centre, without losing its aura. It was an important lesson for cities wishing to remain frozen in time.

Across the Pyrenees, the Barcelona Olympics and the Seville Expo—including the Puerto Rico Pavilion—became instant locales of architectural pilgrimage, and we paid homage to both. A group of us even crossed the Strait of Gibraltar to Tangier, where we ate couscous with our hands and read Paul Bowles' Sheltering Sky. Throughout its beautiful pages, the author made a compelling and eloquent distinction between tourists and travelers. Surely, we were the latter.

Near the end of my Parisian sojourn, I entered the *William Van Alen International Student Design Competition* while still working on the design studio project. That year's challenge asked for a solution to the still unfinished Sagrada Familia church by Antoni Gaudí, and I was fortunate to have visited it at least a couple of times. With no laptops or computers, I actually used a T-Square in my room's old wooden desk and somehow sent a pair of vellum sheets to New York, where a jury awarded me the Second Prize. It was the beginning of a life-long affair with design competitions.

Upon my return to San Juan, I decided to take a gap year

between the Bachelor's and Master's degrees. I interned at the offices of Jorge Rigau and Héctor Arce, Puerto Rican Cornellians who shared Colin Rowe's passion for the city and its history. Both Jorge and Héctor required attention to detail, drawing "like the gods on the Olympus" and a commitment to architecture as an intellectual discipline that transcended required courses and carried beyond nine to five work hours. I am immensely indebted to both. My decision to pursue an academic career probably had its genesis in those memorable studios in Miramar and Santurce.

Back then, my mother worked with the Conservation Trust of Puerto Rico, a world-class organization led by architect Francisco Javier Blanco. The *Fideicomiso*, as it was commonly known, was dedicated to preserving Puerto Rico's natural and cultural heritage, including some of its most significant architectural icons. I grew up visiting its properties and witnessing the various processes through which they were rescued and transformed, appreciating the value of history, culture, and conservation within el Faro, la Buena Vista, la Esperanza, and la Casa Power y Giralt in Old San Juan. Architecture was more than just designing new buildings.

Both Arce and Blanco had attended Harvard's GSD for their graduate degrees and enthusiastically recommended me in that direction. Admittedly, I was astounded when the admission letter arrived. I loved Cambridge and Boston, walking around its beautiful neighborhoods and being exposed to the incredibly diverse and international community I found there. At Gund Hall, I was fortunate to interact with and learn from an

FRANCISCO J. RODRÍGUEZ-SUÁREZ

astonishing collection of inspiring professors. Upon graduation, I stayed in Boston, working at Machado & Silvetti, where I literally received a second graduate education and met some of my dearest and most trusted colleagues.

While at the GSD, I received a Fulbright Fellowship in Spain to conduct research for my thesis under the guidance of Gabriel Ruiz Cabrero, who oversaw the restoration at the Mezquita de Córdoba. Six years after that memorable summer, I returned to a city that had become a second home. The rest of the Fulbright community was predominantly composed of historians and anthropologists from whom I learned about archives and the creation of knowledge. Towards the end of the year, I attended the UIA Congress in Barcelona, where I met Andrés Mignucci, a talented architect from Puerto Rico who would become one of my best friends and colleagues.

In 1999, I returned to San Juan with the intention of teaching at the UPR. Those days at the Río Piedras campus bring back wonderful memories marked by intense creative energy. After a few years, I was offered the role of Undergraduate Program Coordinator. It was my first academic administrative position, but it would not be my last. After the current Dean retired, I was lured by Segundo Cardona into submitting my candidacy. Originally, I was hesitant, only thirty-five years old, with two young boys and a promising practice. Eventually, after discussing the matter with friends and colleagues, I decided to throw my name into the hat.

As Dean, I still taught the Competition Studio, edited

publications, organized strategic collaborations, and designed the new university logo. Fellow Dean Jorge Rodríguez-Beruff became an academic mentor of sorts. Together, we discussed the role and relevance of the public university in the twenty-first century. Those memorable conversations resulted in the publication of *Aula Magna* and *Alma Mater*, and also *Chronologies of an Architectural Pedagogy*. At the end of my tenure, I was the longest-serving Dean on the eleven-campus system but still the youngest. I had presided over the Academic Senate during a strike and was even nominated to be Chancellor and President of the university.

Another presidency provided a new adventure in my life: ACSA—the *Association of Collegiate Schools of Architecture* in Washington, DC. It was a challenging task, as I had to juggle my role on the board in the aftermath of Hurricane Maria in Puerto Rico, where we spent almost six months without electricity. Working together with great colleagues, I was proud to have passed the first political motion condemning the construction of Trump's border wall. I lobbied for architecture to be considered a STEM discipline. Even though I had promised myself not to consider another administrative experience, the years at ACSA planted the seed for a series of ideas and initiatives that merited another chance.

In 2019, I accepted the directorship at Illinois, the oldest public school of architecture in the U.S. Rebecca and I moved to Urbana's Erlanger House in January of 2020, shortly after a series of earthquakes in Puerto Rico and a few months before the first cases of the global COVID pandemic. I have never been too proud of utilizing the term *resilient* as a positive quality. Still, after dealing with strikes, economic crises, hurricanes, and earthquakes, we were ready for another challenge. Thankfully, the university acted correctly, with leadership and an appreciation of science, making tough decisions that paved the way for many scientific and academic innovations.

While the school's remarkable history originally enamored me, admittedly, I was also intrigued by its astonishing potential in a new millennium. Moreover, I was also inspired by the possibility of designing pathways that sought a unifying paradigm between memory and desire as we turned toward the future for new answers. This fundamental distinction was essential to draw the initial lines in the collective canvas of our academic community's imagination, framing the ISoA as an epicenter of design, research, and innovation aimed at solving contemporary society's most pressing challenges, such as global warming, housing inequities, and sustainable communities.

Throughout my directorship of the ISoA, I have prioritized our presence in Chicago, arguably one of the epicenters of architecture culture and production, by creating an Alumni Advisory Board, the ABC studio, and an innovative professional collaboration with the most important architecture firms in the city. I have also stressed an international agenda that includes previously underserved locales in Africa, Asia, Latin America, and the Caribbean. As a matter of fact, a significant percentage of our recent Plym and Pelli Distinguished Visiting Professors have represented those areas, including the first Native American woman to do so.

One of the crucial challenges posed by today's academia is the possibility of moving at the speed of innovation and changes posed by the new millennium. As a director, I have paved the way for the ISoA to remain both flexible and relevant. I have also repositioned the ISoA at the forefront of the academic and professional discourse, expanding our international footprint and relevance, finally designing and building bridges and collaborations between our program and a more connected world than ever.

Every morning I have a cup of Puerto Rican coffee, I tackle a previously printed sudoku, and then I turn the piece of paper around to sketch for a few minutes. It is a necessary routine where I frame the day and its collection of challenges and possibilities. I still draw in napkins and any piece of paper I can get my hands on. Ultimately, when you love what you do, every day is both a workday and a vacation day, and the period between nine to five is only an organizational suggestion.

UNA COSITA MÁS

Interestingly, most of my clients tend to admit they are frustrated architects. I, on the other hand, am a frustrated writer. Theorist Dave Hickey used to say that art was fast and cheap, and architecture was slow and expensive. Consequently, it took two different people to engage each discipline successfully. On the other hand, I have found a convenient marriage between my passion for architecture and my love for the written word. They are two ways of dreaming, perhaps of the same dream.

In the end, I am convinced our challenge is arguably to leave places and spaces in a better state than how we found them, whether that is an existing building, a public space, a community, or an institution like a school of architecture, always searching for that unifying paradigm between theory and practice; again, the hybrid.

After many years, I realized that I wasn't going to be the best architect, the best professor, the best writer, or the best academic administrator. Still, I had the unique possibility of playing all those roles at a very high level. I get immense pleasure and a sense of accomplishment doing so.

I think that was also the case with my mentors Javier Blanco, Héctor Arce, and Andrés Mignucci. They are no longer with us, but I think about them every day, hoping that I can make a difference the way they did, mentoring the next generation and leaving things better than how I found them.

BIOGRAPHY

Francisco J. Rodríguez-Suárez, FAIA was born in San Juan, Puerto Rico in 1970. He is currently the Director of the University of Illinois School of Architecture at Urbana-Champaign. Prof. Rodríguez-Suárez studied architecture at Georgia Tech, the Université de Paris, and Harvard GSD, where he earned a Master of Architecture with Distinction winning the AIA Medal, the Fulbright Fellowship and the Portfolio Award.

In 2017, he was elected president of the Association of Collegiate Schools of Architecture (ACSA), an organization that had previously recognized him as Distinguished Professor. As ACSA president, he lobbied for architecture to be included as a STEM discipline and organized an international congress in Madrid to discuss the future of architectural pedagogy. In 2019, he was inducted into the American Institute of Architects College of Fellows, and in 2020, his peers elected him Chairman of the ACSA College of Distinguished Professors.

During his tenure as director, Rodríguez-Suárez has transformed the Illinois School of Architecture's curriculum and faculty, aspiring for a more diverse community with a sustained presence in Chicago and Barcelona. He organized the first all-female lecture series, as well as one totally dedicated to voices from the Global South. He is committed to facilitating the process for the ISoA to become a partner with communities within the state of Illinois, convinced that architecture could make a profound difference in their spatial and cultural environments.

Paco, as he is known to most, has also taught and lectured at prestigious universities in Europe, Asia, Latin America, Africa, the US, Canada, the Middle East, and the Caribbean, including a sojourn as Visiting Scholar at the American Academy in Rome and a Fulbright Fellowship in Spain.

Before Illinois, he previously spent twenty years at the Universidad de Puerto Rico, half of which he served as Dean. At UPR, Francisco directed (in)forma, an award-winning academic journal, founded CIUDAD, an urban think tank, and co-edited five books including *Alma Mater, Aula Magna, Chronologies of an Architectural Pedagogy, and Contemporary Architecture in Puerto Rico 1992-2010,* a joint effort with the *American Institute of Architects.*

Rodríguez-Suárez has earned over ten AIA Awards and Citations, several Bienal awards in seven different categories, and has been widely published and exhibited worldwide. Francisco was selected by El Nuevo Día newspaper as one of the ten most influential pioneers for 2008, when he collaborated with artist Ai Wei Wei on the Ordos 100 project in China.

Francisco Rodríguez-Suárez

paco70@illinois.edu

One of my favorite sketches because it was all done with a single line.

Alicia Ponce AIA, NCARB, LEED AP BD+C

ABOUT THE AUTHOR

A registered architect in Illinois and Wisconsin, Alicia Ponce is the founder and principal of APMonarch, a Chicago-based female- and Latina-owned architecture firm. Her expertise and passion to design healthy buildings and equitable communities have supported many clients in designing radically better projects. Under Alicia's direction, the firm provides architectural services, sustainability consulting, and community engagement for projects in the Midwest and Latin America. We are open for contracts.

Alicia refers to APMonarch as the pollinators of the built environment, designing healthy environments that look good, feel good, and perform great. She believes that everyone should have a right to a space that brings them comfort and joy. Her reputation for resilient and nature-inspired architecture provides her clients with architecture that is ambitious, thoughtful, and healthy. Notable projects include Exelon, The Field Museum, the University of Chicago Keller Center, Midway International Airport Concessions and Centro Amazing in Aguascalientes, Mexico.

Alicia currently serves on the Chicago Landmarks Commission, is on the board of United Way Metro Chicago, and is the founder of Arquitina, a national non-profit with a mission to raise the fewer than 1% of licensed Latina architects in the United States.

Made in USA - Kendallville, IN
88281_9781957058900
03.18.2024 1340